GANDHIAN HOLISTIC ECONOMICS

Gandhian Studies and Peace Research Series

1. Gandhian Model of Development and World Peace
   R.P. Misra (ed.)
2. Conflict Resolution Through Non-Violence: Role of the Universities, Vol. I: Science and Ethics
   K.D. Gangrade and **R.P. Misra** (eds.)
3. Conflict Resolution Through Non-Violence: Role of the Universities, Vol. 2: Development without Destruction
   K.D. Gangrade and **R.P. Misra** (eds.)
4. The Social Philosophy of Mahatma Gandhi
   K.S. Bharathi
5. Gandhian Humanism
   Mohit Chakrabarti
6. Gandhian Holistic Economics
   Shashi Prabha Sharma

ABOUT THE AUTHOR

DR. SHASHI PRABHA SHARMA is Senior Lecturer of Economics at Daulat Ram College, Delhi University. Educated at Punjab, Haryana and Delhi, she took her Ph.D in Economics in 1988. She has been teaching Statistics, Economic theory and comparative Economic Development.

Dr. Sharma is a scholar of varied interests. She is deeply interested in the study of Philosophy, Psychology and metaphysical matters. It was her interest in the ultimate issues that made her delve deep in the philosophical foundations of economics. Mahatma Gandhi's ideology of 'truth' and 'non-violence' is her special field. Dr. Sharma is of the view that Gandhian economics which stems from holistic foundations and moves within the framework of 'truth' and 'non-violence' is the only hope of the modern disturbed world. She has contributed numerous articles in learned journals on the subject.

Gandhian Studies and Peace Research Series: 6

GANDHIAN HOLISTIC ECONOMICS

SHASHI PRABHA SHARMA
Department of Economics
Daulat Ram College
University of Delhi, Delhi

CONCEPT PUBLISHING COMPANY, NEW DELHI 110059

ISBN 81-7022-446-2

First Published 1992

Published and Printed by
Ashok Kumar Mittal
Concept Publishing Company
A/15-16, Commercial Block, Mohan Garden
NEW DELHI 110059 (India)

Lasertypeset by
Microtech Advance Printing Systems (Pvt.) Ltd.
H-13, Bali Nagar
NEW DELHI 110015

DEDICATED

TO

THE MEMORY

OF

MY PARENTS

PREFACE

> "My life is one indivisible whole and all my activities run into one another and they all have their rise in my insatiable love for mankind."
>
> **M.K. Gandhi**, *Harijan*, March 2, 1934

MODERN WORLD is marked by an economic crisis, enveloping not only the economic but also the individual, social, political and environmental life of man. The pursuit of materialism with all its emphasis on growth and development has led neither to individual happiness nor to social harmony and peace. Man lives in a state of inner contradictions and outer disconnections being placed against man, society and nature. The problems of poverty and hunger, unemployment and inflation are assuming staggering proportions day-by-dav. Threats of environmental pollution, depleting resources, and deteriorating ecological balance loom wider than ever before. The insatiable demand for world resources and markets has led to a systematic draining of the 'third world' countries and has added to political tensions resulting in mounting defence expenditures and fierce race for armament.

The problems act and react upon one another, have positive feed-back loops, and are global in character. The conventional economic tools and institutions are proving of no avail in dealing with the situation; the complexity and magnitude of the problems are growing continuously. It is being fast realised that if the present trends continue unaltered, the limits to growth on this planet would soon be reached, and that the very industrial system might collapse endangering human survival.

The present chaotic disorder calls into question the very foundations on which economics is based, necessitating an alternative approach. The study of meta-economic factors, the world-view, and value system motivating human behaviour can no longer be ignored when inherent contradictions are threatening to destroy the entire economic system. The restructuring of economics on alternative foundations is urgently required for 'peace' and 'permanence'.

Gandhian economics is based on a paradigm that is fundamentally different from that which forms the basis of the prevailing economics. The present work is being undertaken to present a philosophical analysis of Gandhian economics. It is proposed to explore the Gandhian paradigm, the value-system and the concepts, and examine how they bear upon economic principles, policies, analysis and structures, with special reference to the solution of the existing economic problems.

Gandhiji was not an economist in the conventional sense of the term, who wrote book especially on economics. Gandhian economic ideas are scattered throughout his vast and voluminous literature of writings, speeches and letters. The purpose of this research work is to pick out the Gandhian economic ideas, put them in a systematic order and examine the philosophical rationale behind them.

The work is divided into six chapters. The first chapter discusses the relationship between the world-view held by a society at a particular time and the prevailing economics. The paradigm underlying modern economics is examined in the second chapter. The influence of the prevailing 'fragmentary' world-view on modern economic thought, classical, neo-classical, Keynesian and Marxian is analysed, especially from the point of view of the concept of man and society, the economic values, rational economic behaviour, concept of growth, methods of production, inherent contradictions in the socio-economic order, and the nature of the solution of economic problems. The third chapter deals with the world economic crisis generated by the fragmentary paradigm underlying modern economics. An analysis of the world economic problems has been undertaken, followed by a discussion of the failure of modern economic tools to deal with them, thus establishing the need for an alternative paradigm. The fourth chapter takes up the Gandhian 'holistic' paradigm, dealing purely with the philosophy of Mahatma Gandhi, which is the bedrock of all his economic thought. The meaning and concept of wholeness, the concept of man and society, the emanating values, Truth as the goal of life and love or non-violence as the means, have been analytically examined. Founded upon 'holistic' grounds, the economic 'ends' set forth by Gandhiji have been examined in the fifth chapter. The economic 'ends' based upon Truth can be achieved by 'holistic' means only because there is an inviolable connection between 'ends' and 'means'. The sixth chapter deals with a philosophical analysis of the Gandhian holistic 'means', methods of production and distribution, economic structure and policy, with special reference to the dynamics of social and economic change.

The subject has been specifically dealt with from the following points of view:

(a) The philosophical foundations of Gandhian economics *vis-a-vis* those of modern economics,
(b) Comparative study of the values, the concept of man and society, the purpose of economics, the concept of growth, 'ends' and 'means' adopted by the two approaches,
(c) The link between present economic problems and the paradigm underlying modern economics,
(d) A philosophical analysis of Gandhian economic principles, concepts, structure and solutions to economic problems, and
(e) The dynamics of Gandhian change.

The prevailing economic crisis is rooted in the 'fragmentary' paradigm underlying modern economics. Mahatma Gandhi takes a 'holistic' world-view and perceives life as an organic, whole. Founded on 'holistic' grounds and moving within the basic values of 'truth' and non-violence, Gandhian economic ideas represent an extremely systematic, coherent and logical economic system, showing a radical departure from modern economics. Gandhian holistic economics offers a solution to the present-day economic problems, assuring peace, prosperity and progress. It will be no exaggeration to say that Mahatma Gandhi was an economist, who constructed his economic ideas with the rationality of a scientist and the love of a saint.

SHASHI PRABHA SHARMA

ACKNOWLEDGEMENTS

I EXPRESS my deep regard and sincere gratitude to Ms. Vimala Thakar, the sole inspiration behind this work.

I sincerely thank my supervisor, Prof. P.C. Jain, Chairman of the Department of Economics, Kurukshetra University, without whose valuable advice and expert guidance, this work would not have materialised.

I shall remain in deep gratitude to late Shri Jainendra Kumar for illuminating discussions on the philosophy of Mahatma Gandhi.

I tender my sincere thanks to Dr. J.D. Sethi, Professor, Delhi School of Economics, and Dr. Ramashray Roy, Senior Research Fellow, Centre for the Study of Developing Societies, Delhi, for their invaluable suggestions and enriching discussions.

My special thanks are due to Dr. K.L. Krishan, Professor, Delhi School of Economics, for kind guidance, help and encouragement.

I am in gratitude to late Shri N.K. Pant, who was Honorary Secretary, Gandhi Bhawan, Delhi University, for encouragement and helpful discussions.

I am highly obliged to Shri T.S. Ananthu, Research Fellow, Gandhi Peace Foundation, New Delhi, for organising a workshop on 'Resurgence of Gandhian World-view', and enlightening discussions on the latest developments in science.

I would like to specially thank my friend Dr. Barbara Pennington for stimulating conversations, absorbing discussions and helpful advice.

I am highly thankful to Prof. R.P. Mishra, Director, Gandhi Bhavan, Delhi, for help and guidance in the publication of the book.

I am thankful to Dr. Harish Naval and Mrs. Ravinder P. Singh who willingly lent active support, help and cooperation.

I express sincere thanks and deep gratitude to my College Principal Dr. (Mrs.) Deepali Chandra, and ex-Principal Dr. (Mrs.) S.K. Nambiar, for encouraging and granting me study leave.

My thanks are due to the officials at Sevagram Ashram and Pawnar Ashram, who made my visit to these places a success and helped me in collecting valuable information and material.

I owe my thanks to the staff of: Gandhi Bhavan Library, Delhi University; Ratan Tata Library, Delhi School of Economics; Gandhi Museum and Library, New Delhi; Gandhi Peace Foundation Library, New Delhi; and Daulat Ram College Library, Delhi.

I extend my sincere thanks to all my friends, colleagues and relatives, who have helped and encouraged me in this study.

I specially thank my brothers Alok, Arvind and Ashok, who constantly encouraged and urged me on to complete the work.

Last but not least, I thank my husband O.P. Sharma and children Vikas and Sonal, who have not only tolerated my busy pursuit with utmost patience for a long period, but have also encouraged, cooperated and assisted me in umpteen ways.

SHASHI PRABHA SHARMA

CONTENTS

1

WORLD-VIEW AND ECONOMICS

ECONOMICS ALWAYS grows out of a world-view held by the society consciously or unconsciously at a particular time. The concepts and values a society lives by are determined by the vision or perception of the ultimate reality of life. These concepts and values of life in their turn influence the basic economic values which bear upon the shape and direction of economic thought implicitly or explicitly. The entire economic structure, the principles, policy, analysis and all the other economic manifestations rest upon the bedrock of postulates regarding the ultimate reality of life. The influence of a particular world-view and the basic economic values accompanying it has always been reflected in the writings of the economists of all ages.

The world-view of a particular time is the view regarding the ultimate realities of existence. It enquires into the ultimate nature of the universe, the ultimate immutable reality that is the substratum of this apparently mutable world. All human action springs from a particular 'paradigm' that is the vision or perception of a reality. Man has always wondered at the ultimate essence and purpose of life. Every individual has a particular view regarding his own self and surroundings consciously or unconsciously. This view is the motivational force of human behaviour. There are basically three sources of knowledge: Spirituality, Philosophy and Science, which go into the framing of the world-view, the paradigm prevailing at a particular time. According to I.K. Taimni, "All the three branches of knowledge mentioned above: Religion, Philosophy and Science — take it as an axiomatic truth that there is an ultimate reality underlying the universe and all facts of existence. Conceptions with regard to the nature of this reality may differ, methods of finding that reality may vary, but there is no difference of opinion as far as the existence of such a reality is concerned".[1]

Spirituality, Philosophy, and Science

Spirituality is an ingoing non-cerebral activity for investigating the nature of reality. The mind is allowed to go into a complete abeyance and the intelligence concealed in silence conducts the enquiry and reveals the knowledge regarding the Absolute. In the moments of complete silence and absolute purity of mind Truth reveals itself as it is. Sometimes, there is sudden flash of enlightenment and sometimes the revelation takes place gradually as an intuitive perception. All the religions have always accepted revelations as the supreme source of knowledge. In all organised religions, their founders, prophets and messengers are declared to have gone into supersensuous state of mind and to have come face to face with a new series of facts. All their teachings came through this, and not through intellectual cogitations.[2] The opening verses of the first chapter of Rishi Patanjali's *Yog-Darshan* maintain that we see that real nature of our being with a mind which is calm, all its modifications having been controlled. The great scientist Einstein has attributed the creative faculty to the visionary insight that he terms as 'The cosmic religious experience'. He says, "I do not arrive at my understanding of the fundamental laws of the universe through my rational mind. . . . The cosmic religious experience is the strongest and the noblest mainspring of scientific research."[3] In modern times, internationally renowned philosopher, J. Krishnamurti, has said, "That state of mind which is no longer capable of striving is the true religious mind, and in that state of mind you may come upon this thing called truth or reality or bliss or God or beauty or love."[4]

Philosophy makes certain basic assumptions regarding the ultimate reality of life. From these basic assumptions with the help of deductive logic and common worldly experience a system of thought is spun out explaining the nature of the universe and human existence. The systematised thought further acts as a guide to human conduct. The philosophers are either men of some mystic or occult experience or borrow their ideas from the revelations made in religion. In this way, philosophy points out to the truth of life to a certain extent with the help of reason based on certain fundamental assumptions.

Science, on the other hand, adopts the inductive method of enquiry for the discovery of truth. It makes a basic assumption regarding the objectivity of mind and consciousness. Experiments are held in a particular field of enquiry and data is accumulated. When sufficient data are available, these are analysed to discover the law underlying and a hypothesis is formulated which can account satisfactorily for the observed facts. Further experimentation is held to test the hypothesis, corrections, if necessary, are made, and ultimately, a theory is established having a universal applicability. Science, in this way, uses the faculties of brain, on the one hand, and external matter on the other — as instruments for its investigation. A theory may also be formulated on the basis of data already available as a result of earlier experimentations by others. Science thus discovers the truth of our worldly existence and adds to the knowledge of mankind.

What Economics is Concerned With ?

A close look at the various definitions of economics shows that economics is basically concerned with man's behaviour in the realm of goods and services. For Adam Smith and his followers, economics was a science of man's efforts regarding acquisition of wealth. 'An Enquiry into the Nature and Causes of Wealth' for Adam Smith was of paramount importance because he believed, "Every man is rich or poor according to the degree in which he can afford to enjoy the necessaries, conveniences, and amusements of human life".[5] Thus, according to Adam Smith, economics is concerned with the accumulation of commodities that man may enjoy. Marshall highlighted man's actions and defined economics as "A study of mankind in the ordinary business of life; it examines that part of the individual and social action which is most closely connected with the attainment and with use of the material requisites of well being". For, Marshal, economics studies human actions in relation to material means or requisites of welfare. Pigou also looks at economics as the study of human action related to economic welfare.[7] Prof. Lionel Robbins, in his essay on the 'Nature and Significance of Economic Science', emphasised 'human behaviour' but shifted the focus from 'welfare' to 'scarcity' in the definition of economics. According to Robbins, "Economics is the science which studies human behaviour as a relationship between ends and scarce means which have alternative uses".[8] In recent years, Prof. Samuelson has given a new definition of economics presenting the problem of scarcity in its dynamic context, "Economics is the study of how people and society end up choosing with or without the use of money, to employ scarce productive resources that could have alternative uses — to produce various commodities and distribute them for consumption, now or in the future, among various persons and groups in society".[9] Thus, according to Samuelson also, economics is concerned with human behaviour in dealing with the problem of 'choice' as far as commodities are concerned now or in the future. The subject matter of economics is man's behaviour *vis-a-vis* goods and services. Various aspects of the same problem, have been emphasised by different schools of thought according to the needs of the time. Sometimes it is the total quantum of goods and services called 'wealth' which has been the main concern of the economists and sometimes it is the welfare obtained that has captured their attention. Sometimes, it is the 'scarcity' of goods and services that has been the economic problem and sometimes it is their growth that has served as the coveted target for the economists. Whatever be the focal point of attention, however, there is no denying the fact that economics studies man's behaviour and goods.

The 'Ends' and the 'Means'

How will man behave as far as goods and services are concerned? It is a fundamental question of the concept of man, on the one hand, and the nature of man's relationships with man, society and nature, on the other. The concept of man and the dynamics of his relationship is determined by the view of man about his own 'self' and the 'non-self'. The image regarding the 'self' and the 'non-self' or the 'me' and 'not me' is determined by the explicit or implicit assumption of a particular world-view. The 'self' image determines the purposes or the ends of life which in turn provides motivational force to human activity. The view regarding the 'non-self' determines the nature of man's relationship with the rest of the environment in achieving his ends. The economic ends are shaped by the concept of man or the 'self' image and the purpose of human life, the view regarding relationships gives direction to the 'means' to achieve the 'ends'. The world-view at a particular time thus determines the 'ends' and the 'means' which may be termed as: the warp and the weft of economic thought. The fundamental assumptions regarding the ultimate reality, the concept of man, his environment and their relationship serve as the bedrock of economics. The entire fabric of economics, its concepts, principles, theory and analysis can be seen as stemming from the world-view of a particular time though its influence on man's nature and his relationships within the frame-work of the basic values adopted.

The fact that economic thought operates within the framework of the knowledge of the ultimate issues has always been recognised. James Bonar, publishing his *Philosophy and Political Economy* in 1893 has established that the economic ideas of a particular time always reflect the prevailing philosophy and that the economic thought has always been moulded by changes in philosophical thought. He writes, "Political Economy, or the study of the relation of human society to its material wealth and philosophy or the study of first principles and ultimate issues, have at various times exerted an influence on one another which the history of Economics and Philosophy makes very evident".[10] To prove his contention, Bonar goes on to say, "Economic doctrine as is traceable in the writings of Greek Philosophers grows out of their moral and political philosophy".[11] He has further held, "In medieval and modern times, political economy grows out of political philosophy".[12] Haney has also maintained that a man's whole attitude towards economics as a science is bound to be influenced by his philosophical leanings, whether these be conscious or not. He describes philosophy to be one of the very fundamental factors in determining the course of economic thought, "Back of the different systems of economic thought, or even particular theories, there lie more fundamental factors which condition them and determine their nature and form. The most important of these factors are: (1) the underlying philosophy, and (2) the method of the thinker, which influence his interpretation of economic phenomena and the conclusions which he may draw".[13]

The world-view exerts a deep influence on the psychology or behavioural pattern of man by affecting his image regarding the 'self' and 'non-self'. What a man thinks of himself determines his purposes or targets and the view regarding others affects the means or methods adopted for achieving the same. Psychology, in turn, has its influence on economics since economics studies human behaviour. According to Joseph Schumpeter, "Economics like other social sciences deals with human behaviour. Psychology is really the basis from which any social science must start and in terms of which, all fundamental explanations must run".[14]

E.F. Schumacher has stated that there are 'meta-economic' factors which give direction and shape to the content of economics, "We might say that economics does not stand on its own feet, or that it is a 'derived' body of thought — derived from meta-economics".[15] Regarding the nature of meta-economics, Schumacher explains, "As economics deals with man in his environment, we must expect that meta-economics consists of two parts — one dealing with man and the other dealing with the environment. In other words, we may expect that economics must derive its aims and objectives from a study of man, and that it must derive at least a larger part of its methodology from a study of nature".[16] Thus economic 'ends' and 'means' depend upon meta-economics. E.F. Schumacher has further shown that as the meta-economic basis or the underlying picture of man and nature changes, the conclusions and prescriptions of economics change. He maintains, "Economics is a 'derived' science which accepts instructions from what I call meta-economics. As the instructions are changed, so changes the content of economics".[17]

Relevance of Gandhian Economics

Modern world is faced with a multi-faceted economic crisis entailing poverty in the midst of plenty, insecurity of employment, alienation, erosion of moral values, uncontrolled urbanisation, environmental pollution, depletion of resources, ecological imbalance, inflation and other monetary and economic problems. The efforts to solve the problem by technological progress and exploitation of natural resources are further aggravating the situation. As a matter of fact, the problems are becoming more and more complex and gigantic day by day. One of the most important characteristics of the world economic problems of today is their inter-connectedness and inter-dependence. The problems act and interact upon each other, have positive feedback loops, and are not restricted to national boundaries. All these factors have gone a long way in increasing the magnitude and complexity of the problems. As a result, the traditional fragmentary economic solutions have been rendered quite ineffective in tackling these problems of a complex and global nature. As the Club of Rome holds, "The major problems facing mankind are of such complexity and are so inter-related that traditional institutions and policies are no longer able to cope with them, not even come to grips with their full content".[18]

The current economic crisis with all its complexity calls into question the very foundations of economics. The nature of the pressing economic problems that the world is facing today and the failure of the traditional economics to find a solution to them, necessitates a deep examination of the world-view underlying the entire economic thought.

The solution to our problems cannot be found from within the existing theoretical frame-work, as the roots of the problems lie somewhere outside the system in the paradigm, that bears upon the basic values and concepts of economics. In Schumacher's language, a deep study of meta-economics is required, "The study of economics is too narrow and too fragmentary to lead to valid insights, unless complemented, and completed by a study of meta-economics".[19] The present economic system contains the seeds of its own destruction. If the economic activity continues with the old methodology motivated by the traditional economic drives, the entire economic system is likely to meet a disastrous end. A study team at MIT (U.S.A.), under the guidance of Prof. Dennis Meadows, has concluded, "If the present growth trends in world population, industrialisation, pollution, food production and resource depletion continue unchanged, the limits to growth on this planet will be reached sometimes within the next one hundred years".[20] The restructuring of economics based on a new vision of reality is urgently required. It is in this connection that Gandhian Economics based on a fundamentally different paradigm becomes most relevant. Dr. V.K.R.V. Rao has observed, "Gandhi's ideas are beginning to command increasing attention in a world that is disillusioned by the working of both capitalism and communism and attracted by the possibility that the circle can be squared with economic growth, social justice, full employment, economic and social equality, political democracy, and individual freedoms all forming components of a harmonious new social order".[21]

NOTES

1. I.K. Taimni, *Science and Occultism*, Madras, The Theosophical Publishing House, 1974, pp. v-vi.
2. Vivekananda, *Jnana Yoga*, 14th impression, Calcutta, The Sun Lithography Co., pp. 6-7.
3. Quoted in T.S. Ananthu, *Lecture Notes on New Paradigm emerging from 20th Century Developments in Sciences*, New Delhi, Gandhi Peace Foundation, 1983, p. 11.
4. J. Krishnamurti, *Freedom from the Known*, Edited by Mary Lutyens, New Delhi, B.I. Publications, 1975, p. 122.
5. Adam Smith, *The Wealth of Nations*, New York, The Modern Library, Random House, Inc., 1937, p. 30.
6. Alfred Marshall, *Principles of Economics*, 8th ed., London, Macmillan & Co. Ltd., 1959, p. 1.
7. A.C. Pigou, *Economics of Welfare*, 4th ed., London, Macmillan & Co., Ltd., 1952, pp. 11-12.

8. Lionel Robbins, *An Essay on the Nature and Significance of Economic Science*, 2nd ed., London, Macmillan & Co. Ltd., 1949, p. 16.
9. Paul A. Samuelson, *Economics*, 11th ed., McGraw-Hill (Aucland), 1980, p. 2.
10. James Bonar, *Philosophy and Political Economy*, 2nd impression, London, George Allen and Unwin Ltd., 1967, p. 3.
11. James Bonar, ibid, p. 5.
12. James Bonar, ibid.
13. Lewis H. Haney, *History of Economic Thought*, 4th ed., New York, The Macmillan Company, 1964, p. 12.
14. Joseph Schumpeter, *History of Economic Analysis*, 4th printing, London, George Allen & Unwin Ltd., 1961, p. 27.
15. E.F. Schumacher, *Small is Beautiful*, New Delhi, Radha Krishna, 1977, p. 42.
16. E.F. Schumacher, ibid.
17. E.F. Schumacher, ibid, p. 47.
18. Donella H. Meadows, et al., *The Limits to Growth*, New York, Potomac Associates, 1974, p. X (2nd ed.)
19. E.F. Schumacher, op. cit., p. 47.
20. Donella H. Meadows, et al., op. cit., p. 29.
21. V.K.R.V. Rao, *Indian Socialism*, New Delhi, Concept Publishing Company, 1982, p. 80.

2

PARADIGM UNDERLYING MODERN ECONOMICS

A STUDY of the paradigm underlying modern economics is called for before enquiring into the foundations of Gandhian economies.

Modern economics came to be based on a totally new paradigm following the enlightenment, involving fundamental changes in philosophical outlook, scientific discoveries and technological advancement. The world-view of the middle ages, chiefly dominated by the Greek philosophy and Christianity was rejected and a completely new value system was evolved, displacing the old set of values and norms governing life. It meant far-going modifications in the concept of man the purpose of life, bringing about revolutionary changes in the social and economic order. An entirely different culture emerged based on the new set of values that still dominates our life.

Philosophy and Economics in the Middle Ages

The philosophy that prevailed during the medieval period was of a dualistic nature, accepting a division between the ideal world and the real world, between the eternal and the temporal. The spirit was considered to exist independently of the matter. In his famous 'Doctrine of Ideas', Plato holds that the ideas behind the particulars are the essence, the substantial reality. The ideas are the eternal transcendent reality which exist *a priori* and are independent of the changes characteristic of the appearances.[1] The particular are copies or imperfect representations of the universal ideas. Plato further holds that these ideas constitute a well ordered rational cosmos and to not merely form some disordered chaos. There is an organic inter-relatedness among these ideas and they are finally under the rule of the supreme idea, the idea of the Good, Truth or Reality.[2] Aristotle similarly, held that the universal is prior to the particular in its nature though it is arrived at later by human reasoning. Christianity also believed that there exists a 'Kingdom of Heaven',[3] a higher order, and a higher law than that of the State.

The Greek philosophy and Christianity both referred to the unity of the spirit and a larger order comprising the different parts. Christianity taught a brotherhood which extended beyond community or nation, embracing all classes and races. The church maintained the natural equality of rights among men and held that men may be unequal but only as brothers are. Closely connected with the doctrine of brotherhood was the idea of the joint ownership of property. Plato desired a complete communion embracing not only property but also wives and children.[4] By the law of nature, all things are common and the same as evident by the divine law, for the earth belongs to the Lord and therefore no men can truly say, "This field is mine" or "This house is mine".[5]

It was because of the dualistic philosophy of the medieval period that man was not taken as an independent self-sufficient being defining for himself his ends and selecting means to realise them. The laws and means governing human conduct existed *a priori* being embedded in the higher order. Man was supposed to follow the given rules and obey the heavenly commandments in order to be good and happy. The well-being of human life thus consisted in conforming to the pre-existing rules and regulations.

The realisation of the true Good of all beings is the purpose of man's life. Man, though a limited and imperfect being, has the potentiality to gain true knowledge. Aristotle insists that the foremost duty of every rational being is to pursue the immortal under all circumstances. The Supreme Idea, the Idea of Good can be realised by contemplation and virtuous life. Since God has created every being, life must be based on the law of love and the principle of equality of all beings. The values and norms of life are determined by the principles of higher order and not by the dictates of selfish human nature. A good and virtuous life is essential for spiritual pursuits and is also the source of true happiness. To be happy, one must be good, was therefore a dominant note and the interests of the soul were placed the foremost. "There are in all three things", says Plato, "about which every man has an interest; and the interest about money, when rightly regarded, is the third and lowest of them; midway comes the interest of the body; and first of all that of the soul; and the State which we are describing will have been rightly constituted, if it ordains honours according to this scale'.[6] Jesus had said, "You cannot serve two masters; God and Money. For you will hate one and love the other, or else the other way round".[7]

The economic values, emanating from the prevailing view of life, and the idea of ethics paved the way for a purposive economy with the State existing for the purpose of promoting 'good life'. The individual was primarily the citizen, a citizen who on the one hand, depended upon the State for highest development, and who, on the other hand, by his development promoted the highest good of the whole. The Greeks, therefore, held that a certain amount of material resources are essential for the maintenance of the body and perfect exercise of human faculties, but they were considered as a fixed factor. Wants were to be directed and limited according to certain ideals. Wealth and riches beyond the necessaries were regarded as an evil rather than good because they decrease efficiency and obstruct spiritual pursuits. Great riches were considered to be incompatible with happiness because a rich man cannot be a good man as part of his wealth must be acquired and expended unjustly. Plato had warned a note of caution against both, riches and poverty, "for the one produces luxury and idleness and revolution, the other revolution and meanness and villainy besides".[8]

The Greek thinkers preferred the means provided by nature to fulfil human needs. Agriculture was, therefore, considered to be the most desirable occupation. Exchange including commerce, usury and services for hire were not considered natural and, therefore, decried, Furthermore, dignity of labour was recognised; those who ate their bread in the sweat of their faces were appreciated. Economics, during the medieval era was, therefore, concerned with promoting a good and happy life of the people according to the norms and values of the higher order. Haney has given a befitting definition of economics prevailing in those days, "Economics is the science which deals with the satisfaction of human wants through exchange, seeking so to regulate the industries of the State as to make its citizens good and happy and so promote the highest well-being of the whole".[9]

The Enlightenment

The seventeenth century witnessed the rejection of the world-view which accepted a dualistic philosophy and made happiness and the Idea of Good, the pursuit of human life. The age of reason and scientific inventions led man to snap ties with the Higher Order, a transcendent reality depending upon Faith for its existence. Now there being not binding force of life, man emerged as an independent autonomous being taking his own decisions and bearing the responsibility for his actions. The new world-view accepted life to be in fragments and established man as a material being seeking pleasure. The enlightenment gave a different meaning and direction to life. An entirely new set of values was evolved which bearing upon the economic ideology and human relationships gave rise to what is known as 'modern economics'. The provision of more and more material goods became the sole purpose of the new economics and the independent individual action emerged as the means to achieve the cherished goal. Materialism and individualism became the two main planks on which rested the economics of the early naturalists. The *laisses faire* economics was supposed to lead to the collective good. However, as history rolled by, contradictions appeared in the system and the incompatibility between individual action and social ends could no longer be ignored. Consequently, two different approaches appeared and offered modifications in the economic system of the naturalists. The first approach advocated the intervention of the State at the micro level as well as at the macro level asking for a partial and selective control of the individual action. The second approach found fault with the social and economic relationships. This is noteworthy that the basic paradigm underlying economics remains intact. Both the schools believe in a fragmentary world-view taking man to be a pleasure seeker. The goal of economics as the pursuit of materialism, remains to be the same; it is only the individualism as the means to achieve the goal that is being called into question.

The Fragmentary World-View

The world-view underlying modern economics takes life to be in fragments, accepting that the universe is a system composed of different parts. The various constituents are finite and limited in their existence. The different parts have no inherent movement in them, they behave in a deterministic way moving under some kind of force and thus being mechanistic in nature. Moreover, the different units constituting the universe, living or non-living, are discrete and independent. There is no binding reality underlying them.

The views of Nicolas Copernicus regarding the planetary system and the astronomical discoveries of Galileo Galilie using the newly invented telescope gave a shock to the medieval world-view. However, Cartesian philosophy and the Newtonian physics in the sixteenth and the seventeenth centuries dealt the final blows to the prevailing view of life, completely shattering the old paradigm and marking a beginning for the age of enlightenment. Modern philosophy resting mainly on scientific and rational foundations in contrast to those of faith and intuition in the medieval period, owes its origin to Descartes. He wanted to build a philosophy of life about which there was complete certainty and which like mathematics was based on self-evident truth. Descartes, therefore, wrote, "We reject all knowledge which is merely probable and judge that only those things should be believed which are perfectly known and about which there can be no doubts".[10] In order to arrive at the true nature of things, Descartes begins with doubt, he doubts everything that he can manage to doubt, all traditional knowledge, even his body, senses and feelings. Ultimately, he discovered that all things may be doubtful but the fact that we doubt is not doubtful. Therefore, there is one thing that cannot be doubted, that is our existence as a doubter or thinker. And so, Descartes arrived at his celebrated statement, "Cogito ergo sum", 'I think, therefore I am'.[11] From the fact of thinking, Descartes deduced that thought is the essence of human nature and that all things that we conceive very clearly and very distinctly are true.

Mind was more certain, for Descartes, than matter and therefore he concluded that the two were separate and fundamentally different. Moreover, he took them to be absolutely independent of each other, incapable of influencing each other in any way. The division between mind and matter meant that man is an isolated ego existing inside his body. Descartes takes the self in its God as an Infinite individual state and further takes God as an Infinite. Being, outside the finite self. The mind and body are different from each other, but both are dependent on the supreme substance God. God has created the world and the bodies are moved by Him for they have no capacity for independent motion; they are passive and inert. Mind and body are running parallel to each other like two well adjusted clocks which show the same time though they do not influence each other in any way.[12] Moreover, bodies and all physical things move according to the mechanical laws and Descartes, therefore, further maintains that everything in the material world could be explained in terms of the arrangements and movements of its parts. Descartes does not think that God interferes with the mechanistic system of the world. God endowed the world with a certain amount of motion and rest at the time of creation and He confines himself to the operation of matter within the limits prescribed by Himself originally.

There is no purpose or final cause determining the ways of the world; it merely functions according to the laws of mechanics. Descartes extended his mechanistic view of matter even to living organisms and held that they were nothing but automata. Even the human body, though organic in nature, is mechanical in its function and is moved by the heat generated in the heart. The body functions not purposively but automatically like a machine. "I do not recognise any difference between the machines made by craftsmen and the various bodies that nature alone composes".[13] Descartes thus takes a fragmentary, mechanistic and deterministic view of the world.

Issac Newton earned the credit for completing the Scientific Revolution, started by Copernicus, Kepler, Bacon, Galileo and Descartes. He invented a completely new branch of mathematics, now know as differential calculus and used the same to formulate the exact laws of motion for all objects in the solar system under the influence of the force of gravity. Newton thus developed a complete mathematical formulation of the mechanistic view of nature. As the famous physicist Capra has put it, "The Newtonian Universe was indeed one huge mechanical system, operating according to exact mathematical laws".[14]

According to the Newtonian physics, the ultimate constituents of all matter were material particles, the atoms which were small, solid and indestructible objects. Regarding the nature of these basic building blocks of matter, Capra writes, "Newton assumed matter to be homogeneous; he explained the difference between one type of matter and another not in terms of atoms of different weights but in terms of more or less dense packing of atoms. The basic building blocks of matter could be of different sizes but consisted of the same 'stuff' and the total amount of material substance in an object was given by the object's mass".[15] The motion of material particles or any other material object is caused by the force of gravity according to fixed laws. Therefore, all that happened had a definite cause and gave rise to a definite effect. The future of any part of the system could be predicted with absolute certainty if its state at any time was known in all details. The universe was, therefore, a huge mechanical system running according to the Newtonian laws of motion. Matter was thus thought to be the only basis of all existence and the material world was seen as a multitude of fragmented discrete objects assembled into a huge machine working according to certain fixed laws. As a consequence, all problems could be understood by breaking them into parts studying the mechanism through which they interacted. 'Reductionism' thus became the basic method for understanding complex phenomena.

The Concept of Man and Society

The new developments in physics and philosophy influenced the Sciences of human nature and human society. A new concept of man and society emerged. The famous philosopher, John Locke, developed an atomistic view of society, describing it in terms of its basic element or building block, the human being. Society was taken as a multitude of finite, self-sufficing, autonomous individuals functioning mechanically under some kind of force. There was supposed to be no binding force or spirit underlying the apparently separate individuals. Hobbes observed that the original state of men is a state of isolation, they are separate atoms and that their union is not a natural but a purely artificial one.[16] Thus, the acceptance of a purely rational, mechanistic approach and rejection of an all-encompassing reality led to a basic division between the 'part' and the rest of the world, 'self' and the 'non-self'.

Man was taken as a material being moving in the world of matter strictly governed by the laws of matter. The materialist tendency not only regarded matter as existing independently of mind but went to the extent of denying the existence of anything but matter.[17] John Locke held that the mind has no private truths and therefore described the mind originally as a *tabula rasa*, a blank tablet, on which external objects make their impressions through the senses. The mind cannot have its own ideas independent of sense-perceptions. Ideas come into existence only through the senses as stimulated by matter.

The Pleasure Principle and Possession of More and More

The driving force of human action is the force of self-interest manifesting itself in the pursuit of pleasure or the release of uneasiness. Everybody is always moved in action, solely by desire for his own happiness or pleasure and therefore Locke concluded, "Things are good or evil only in relation to pleasure or pain. That we call 'good' which is apt to cause or increase pleasure, or diminish pain in us".[18] There is natural impulse in man to seek material goods to fulfil his basic needs for the preservation of the body. The contact with the worldly objects creates in man the sensations of pleasure and pain. Now the self-interest drives man to seek pleasure and avoid pain. There is a psychological dimension of pleasure also in addition to that of the sensual. The separation from the Infinite created a void within man which he is forever trying to fill up by making constant efforts for expanding the finite self by possessing more and more. The 'I' lives in a constant fear of annihilation and so there is a natural tendency in man to be acquisitive, protective and therefore competitive. Man gets pleasure not only in acquiring more and more but also in acquiring more than others. Self-interest in this way through the mechanism of sensual and psychological pleasure becomes the prime driving force of human action. As Lutz and Lux have put it, "The behaviour of a human being is a mechanical, automatic and inevitable reaction to forces and causes outside the person's conscious control".[19]

The Positivist View

the fragmentary materialistic world-view means that man is forever caught up in the mechanics of nature. Matter being the ultimate reality, there is no possibility of transcending the mechanistic structure of mind and body. Consequently, it was found irrelevant to study man as he 'ought to be' and attention was focussed on the study of man as he 'is'. Man was taken as a given object having a definite or positive behaviour. The positivist view of man further meant that progress was possible only in the realm of matter. Progress was thus taken as growth in the dimension of matter and acquisition of more and more became the purpose of human life.

Inherent Contradictions

The acquisitive society with its boundless pursuit of materialism has inherent contradictions. Not only that the 'fragment', the individual, or the group pursuing material self-interest is in perpetual contradiction due to the problem of choice, it is placed against nature as well as society. The separation of the 'self' and the 'non-self' leads to a subject and object relationship between the two, the former using the latter completely for its own purpose without any concern for it. This assumes innate violence, the various fragments in pursuit of 'self interest' being in constant collision. Competition at the social and economic level leads to exploitation, aggression, misery and pain. Exploitation of nature also and not only that of man is embedded in the pursuit of self-interest. Nature is looked upon as an object to be bound into service and serve man as a slave. All men are equal as far as their boundless desires are concerned and their will is bounded only by their power. There ensues a struggle for existence with supremacy to the strongest; and it is a struggle which ceases only when the combatants recognise that they are defeating their own ends by continuing it. The State in this way, according to Hobbes, is only a continuance of enlightened selfishness.[20] Social interest becomes necessary only because individual self-interest cannot be served in a state of chaos and disorder. Dr. Ramashray Roy has observed, "It is true that the search for individual happiness compatibly with others becomes necessary for individual well-being and the health of the social order. However, this is only a second order goal considered important for the promotion of the first order goal, i.e., individual happiness".[21]

The Natural Order and Progress

There is a state of natural order in which the different individuals driven by their selfish interests would settle down in a society. John Locke held that by nature men are free and equal and the law of nature wills a liberty that is consistent with the liberty of others. Men know by a natural impulse where their best interest lies and, therefor, nature should be left alone to do her work without any intervention. The faith in the natural order was the seed bed of the policy of *laissez faire.* Men have certain natural rights like life, liberty and the pursuit of happiness. Governments are, therefore, instituted not to impose their laws on the people, but to secure every man the natural rights and the fruits of his labour.

The naturalists further contended that the pursuit of individual self-interest in accordance with the dictates of nature would lead to a state of general good and social benefit. *Laissez faire* does not mean chaos but results in a natural order and progress for all. In 1714, Mandeville published '*The Fable of the Bees*' and at the end of the 'Search into the nature of Society', summed up his conclusion as follows:

> "After this, I flatter myself to have demonstrated that neither the friendly qualities and kind affections that are natural to man, nor

the real virtues he is capable of acquiring by reason and self-denial, are the foundations of society: but that what we call evil in the world, moral as well natural, is the grand principle that makes us sociable creatures, the solid basis, the life and support of all trades and employments without exception: that there we must look for the true origin of all arts and sciences, and that the moment evil ceases the society must be spoiled, if not totally dissolved."[22]

Mandeville thus upheld that 'private vices are public benefits'. David Hume tried to meet the paradoxical situation by asserting that an action is virtuous not vicious if it results in public benefit. The passions as such are not evil for reason cannot lead to action without them.[23] Avarice and luxury are necessary and desirable for national progress.

Charles Darwin's theory of evolution lent further support to the naturalists' views on progress. According to the Darwinian theory, in the struggle for existence, natural selection secures the 'survival of the fittest'.[24] Applying Darwin's theory of biological evolution to society, the Social Darwinists of the nineteenth century believed that progress in society is the result of a struggle for existence ruled by the 'survival of the fittest'. Accordingly, the pursuit of self-interest was glorified and competition was seen as the driving force of society. As Haney has aptly remarked, "The materialists rely upon the blind working of natural selection to bring about a future condition which may be better than the present".[25]

Influence of the Fragmentary Paradigm on Economics

The view regarding the nature of the universe, the concept of man, society and progress held by the scientists and philosophers of the seventeenth and eighteenth centuries is deeply reflected in the entire history of modern economic though. Adam Smith, regarded as the father of modern economics, was profoundly influenced by the view of the philosophers of the time. Regarding those who influenced Smith, the noted economic historian Haney, says, "Adam Smith was acquainted with the writings of the Mercantilists, the philosophers of the seventeenth and eighteenth centuries, and the Physiocrats, and he stood upon their shoulders. The names of Petty, Northchild, Steuart, Locke, Berkeley, Mandeville, Hutcheson, Hume, Tucker and Ferguson must ever be remembered in this connection. Smith also refers to Cantillon and a work by Harris".[26] The fundamental conceptions of

Adam Smith, regarding the natural rights, a beneficent providence and *laissez faire* can be traced in the writings of Hutcheson, who was one of the Smith's teachers at Glasgow, and David hume, one of his greatest friends.

Man as a Material Being Seeking Pleasure

The starting point of Adam Smith's economic thought is the concept of man as a material being seeking pleasure. The purpose of life is enjoyment and, therefore, man always has a desire to "better his conditions" and to live as much at ease as possible. "The desire of bettering our condition, a desire which, though generally calm and dispassionate, comes with us from the womb, and never leaves us till we go into the grave".[27] Smith further asserts that the quality of our life, its richness or poverty depends upon the amount of pleasure that we can manage to obtain. He readily agrees with Cantillon in assuming, "Every man is rich or poor according to the degree in which he can afford to enjoy the necessaries, conveniences and amusements of human life".[28] Smith thus takes it for granted that all men are born 'equal' in the pursuit of pleasure.

In accordance with the prevailing fragmentary world-view, Smith takes man to be an isolated being. Accepting the dichotomy between the 'self' and the 'non-self', he upheld the 'self-interest' as being the prime psychological drive in man. 'Self-love' or 'self-interest' expresses itself in the desire for more and more material goods in order to gain more and more pleasure. Smith, therefore, accepted man to be having unlimited wants. "Human wants and satisfaction were thought of as having a 'natural' tendency uncontrolled by judgements".[29] The material interest of the 'self' assumed supreme importance in life according to the 'natural' philosophy. As John Locke clarified, "We are not born in heaven but in this world, where our being is to be preserved with meat, drink and clothing, and other necessaries that are not born with us, but must be got and kept with forecast, care and labour, and, therefore, we cannot be all devotion, all praises and hallelujah, and perpetually in the vision of things above".[30] Man thus emerged as a consumer dominated by unlimited wants.

Purpose of Economics: Augmentation of Wealth

Man being a bundle of passions and appetites, the purpose of economics is 'augmentation of fortune' or the provisioning of more and more goods for the satisfaction of unlimited desires. Smith was therefore mainly concerned with the annual consumption, the annual necessaries and conveniences of life in a nation. He directed his attention towards 'universal opulence' and augmentation of wealth. The entire 'Wealth of Nations' was written keeping in view the problem of wealth. As Smith has written, "To explain in what has consisted the revenue of the great body of the people or what has been the nature of those funds, which, in different ages and nations, have supplied their annual consumption, is the object of these Four first Books".[31] Adam Smith looked at wealth as power in agreement with Hobbes. He hinted at the possibility of acquiring even political power, civil or military, with wealth. However, he held that the power which the possession of wealth certainly conveys is the power of purchasing, a certain command over all the labour or over all the produce of labour which is then in the market. Therefore, "His fortune is grater or less precisely in proportion to the extent of this power", wrote Smith.[32]

Self-interest Glorified

Smith not only assumed that the prime psychological drive in man is the drive of self-interest, he glorified self-interest by establishing that a society hangs together with the cohesive force of self-interest only. "It is not from the benevolence of the butcher, the brewer or the baker that we expect our dinner, but from their regard to their own interest".[33] He agreed with Mandeville that it is 'self-love' known as 'evil' which is the grand principle that makes us social creatures. There is a natural order in the universe which makes all the individuals striving for self-interest add up to the social good.

Self-interest acts as an economic ordering force through the laws of supply and demand. Smith compared the market mechanism to 'invisible hands' regulating an economy and creating order. The dictates of the market mechanism and the competition resulting from the pursuit of self-interest will lead to the provision of goods that the society wants, at the lowest possible costs. Whenever there is a change in community's desires, production would adjust itself accordingly under the direction of the market mechanism. The producers would just cover their costs and normal profits under the force of competition. The market forces also act as income regulating mechanism. Everybody would be paid according to his or her market price.

Inflation would be a self-curing disease since the market forces would always lead production adjustments in the right direction. The possibility of a part of the labour force being permanently unemployed does not exist. Unemployment simply means that at the going wage rate, there are more workers than the availability of jobs. the wage rate would, therefore, drop until all those who want jobs are employed. An economic system based on private property and free exchange and markets was thus seen by Smith as the only 'natural' way of economic organisation to preserve order and present chaos.

Smith considered self-interest not only essential for the maintenance of the social machinery but also desirable for the development of the economy. Self-interest of the consumer expresses itself in the multiplicity of wants which is essential for providing a market for those who are toiling to produce wealth. "Our passions are the only cause of labour",[34] maintained Hume. Therefore, Smith who assumed labour to be the cause of all physical productivity, found the multiplicity of wants to be of utmost importance for the augmentation of wealth. The division of labour and the accompanying benefits just could not be reaped, without there being a large market for the products of labour. The self-interest of the producer, on the other hand, manifests in competition leading man's creative powers to invent, innovate, expand and take risks.

Since the self-interest of all men adds up to the maximum social good, Smith emphasised that the best policy is *laissez faire*, economic liberalism or non-interventionism, "The natural effort of every individual to better his own condition, when suffered to exert itself with freedom and security, is so powerful a principle that it is alone, and without any assistance, not only capable of carrying on the society to wealth and prosperity, but of surmounting a hundred impertinent obstructions with which the folly of human laws too often incumbers its operation".[35] The wonderful world of Adam Smith led Robert Heilbroner to comment, "The whole complex irrational world is reduced to a kind of rational scheme where human particles are nicely magnetised in a simple polarity towards profit and away from loss. The great system works not because man directs it, but because self-interest and competition line up the filings in the proper way, the most that man can do is to help this natural social magnetism along, to remove whatever barriers stand before the free working out of this social physics, and to cease his misguided efforts to escape from its thralldom".[36]

Smith was suspicious of the activities of the business owners to a certain extent. He apprehended that the landed proprietors as well as capitalists, 'love to reap where they have not sown', that inequality in social position gives masters an advantage in bargaining with their men. His support for division of labour was also not unqualified. He knew that an excessive division of labour might result in dehumanisation of labour. But Smith was mainly concerned with the augmentation of physical productivity. Though sympathetic to the working class, he considered all these evils as a price to be paid for economic development. Moreover, he though that the attempts by the State to keep masters from conspiring in monopolies would probably make a bad situation worse rather than better.

Conflicting Interests

The philosophy of looking at life in fragments leading to the pursuit of unlimited ends determined by the 'self' interest and the use of the 'non-self' as an object to serve as the means to attain the ends has remained to be the same till today since the days of Adam Smith. The fragmentary outlook tended to materialism on the one hand, and individualism, on the other. The pursuit of materialism, though expressed in different forms, permeates the entire history of economic thought. However, individualism as the sole agent leading to the desired goal has not gone without criticism. Mandeville's dictum that 'private vices are social benefits' did not stand the test of time. The pursuit of more and more for the satisfaction of unlimited wants set man against nature without the cooperation of which no production was possible. The multiplicity of wants was found to be faced with the problem of scarcity of resources. Malthus and Ricardo were pioneers in striking pessimistic notes regarding the 'niggardliness of nature'. This led to a fierce competition for the limited world resources, technological advancement in a scientific world and industrial revolution. Consequently, man was set not only against nature but also against man and society. There were inherent contradictions and forces of antagonism in the 'natural' system. As Rousseau observed, the very attempt to grow rich is to find profit in the misfortune of others. Moreover, in a world full of inequalities of possession in income, property, talents and capabilities, the pursuit of self-interest resulting in competition among the unequals leads only to disorder, disharmony and exploitation. The undifferentiated pursuit of materialism in order to fill the 'void' within the self to give it security in a world of finite material resources, accompanied by technological advancement and inequalities of possession led to social imbalances and economic disorder. The nineteenth century witnessed severe poverty, unemployment, exploitation of working class, especially of child and woman labour, and serious problems of booms and depressions. The situation called into question the doctrine of individualism. Two different approaches emerged, one suggesting partial control of the individual and the other, curbing the individual altogether. However, one point was common, both the approaches looked for the villain of the peace in factors external to the 'self'.

Partial Control of the Individual

J.S. Mill was the first economist of the classical tradition to have recognised the evils of the system. He was a utilitarian and believed in the Benthamite philosophy of the greatest happiness of the greatest number. Taking man to be a material being, he accepted pleasure or utility as the purpose of life. However, Mill recognised that the full and ultimate good of the individual lies in the full and ultimate good of his fellows. He accepted man to be a prisoner of the natural environment but regarded civilisation to overcome the limitations of the natural environment and invoked power of the State to ensure social harmony. Side by side, Mill was a strong champion of individual liberty also and held that progress is not possible without every individual being given the chance to develop all his latent talents and faculties. As Haney has given Mills views on liberty, "Individuality, a rich diversity of human development is a source of all progress and should be jealously defended".[37] Mill, therefore, believed in the doctrine of self-interest promoting general welfare and competition as a force of material progress. He, however, was against unbounded and unrestricted liberty to develop one-self, regardless of one's social obligations. Therefore, he held that *laissez faire* in short should be the general practice; every departure from it, unless required by some great good, is a certain evil. It is obvious that in Mill's thought, on the one hand, there is a strong adherence to the pursuit of wealth based on the old *laissez faire* principles and, on the other, a decisive declaration that individualism is to be controlled. It is for this reason that Haney has compared his system "to a Janus head of which the one face looks back into the past, the other forward into the future".[38] Mill distinguished the laws of production from those of distribution, the former being dominated by physical causes, whereas the latter could be determined by mankind, individually or collectively. Mill advocated socialisation of rent by means of a tax on land and lessening of the inequalities of income by a policy of taxation on inheritance. He also suggested associations of workmen to displace the organisations of producers.

Kant, the founder of German Idealism, held that a political government exists to secure the freedom and not the happiness of the people. Each is to seek his own happiness for himself in an atmosphere of freedom secured by the Government.[39] Further, under the sway of Rousseau's thought, German Romanticism implied that each individual personality should be assured the opportunity for self-expression. Each 'self' with its innate and peculiar potentialities must not only be developed but also 'protected' from other selves. The policy of *laissez faire* was not the best under all conditions. However, German romanticism was not reactionary against pursuit of materialism; it merely asked for reforms and suitable state policies to protect the lowly individual or the backward nation.

The Rational Economic Man

The concept of man as a pleasure-seeker with the consumption of more and more goods found new expressions in the writings of Bentham, Karlmenger, Stanley Jevons, Leon Walras and the economists of the neo-classical school. Bentham held that the motivational force behind individual action is the desire for pleasure and dislike for pain. Believing in a hedonistic philosophy, he maintained that human activity is governed by a calculated balancing of pleasures and pains, in other words, the principle of 'utility'. Bentham's Utilitarianism further holds that it is not only that the principle of greatest happiness governs what individuals shall do but also what they ought to do. Since society is just an aggregate of individuals, the interest of the community is merely the sum of the interests of the several members who compose it. Therefore, the guiding principle for government is the principle of the 'greatest good of the greater number'. Utility being the goal of all human action, rational human behaviour lies in utility maximisation. A man acting according to the principle of utility calculation was, therefore, called a 'rational economic man'.

Alfred Marshal, the founder of the neo-classical school, following the utilitarian approach assumed the concept of man as a consumer, making rational calculations of utility. He held "human wants and desires are countless in number and very various in kind".[40] Man desires not merely larger quantities of the things he has been accustomed to consume, but better quality of those things and also wants to satisfy desires arising out of new activities. "Thus though the brute and the savage alike have their preferences for choice morsels, neither of them cares much for variety for its own sake. As, however, man rises in civilisation, as his mind becomes developed and even his animal passions begin to associate themselves with mental activities, his wants rapidly become more subtle and more various and in the minor details of life, he begins to desire change for the sake of change, long before he has consciously escaped from the yoke of custom".[41] Once the desire for change for the sake of change takes its hold on man, needs and wants become unlimited.

The prudent utility maximiser with unlimited wants and limited economic resources has to make rational choices with utmost care. The demand and supply curves clearly reflect the behaviour of the rational economic man. Marshall assumes that each individual buyer has a 'demand schedule' showing an equilibrium between his marginal utility for the good in question and his marginal utility for money. Similarly, the seller of the commodity has a supply schedule representing the equilibrium between the marginal coast and the marginal utility for money. Value is determined at the point of equilibrium between the schedules of 'demand price' and 'supply price'.Economic value is thus determined by the intensity of human desire, the degree of gain in utility or conversely the avoidance of disutility. Apparently, the rational economic behaviour implies the treatment of work, effort and sacrifice of any sort as disutility. Marshall, further applying the principles of demand and supply to determine the price of factors of production treats distribution as a part of the valuation process. People like commodities are supposed to have market valuation.

The behaviour of the rational economic man is extremely fragmentary. He is concerned with the maximisation of gain for the self without any concern for the 'non-self'. the rational calculus of the economic man does not take any account of the damage caused to nature and society. The rational consumer has to buy in the cheapest market for utility maximisation even though some poor sellers being unable to sell their products at competitive prices have to be pushed out of the market. Similarly, the rational producer has to produce at the least possible cost by using the most advanced technology and sell in the dearest market to maximise profits and considers his action justified even though it causes environmental deterioration, exhausts irreplaceable natural resources, displaces labour and ignores the urgent needs of the poor consumers. The mind of the rational economic man is too narrow to encompass any regard or concern for 'others'. As E.F. Schumacher comments, "Neither buyer nor seller is responsible for anything but himself. It would be 'uneconomic' for a wealthy seller to reduce his price to poor customers merely because they are in need or for a wealthy buyer to pay an extra price because the supplier is poor. Equally, it would be 'uneconomic' for a buyer to give preference to home produced goods if imported goods are cheaper. He does not, and is not expected to accept responsibility for the country's balance of payments".[42]

As the rational economic man marched ahead with his pursuit of utility, it became increasingly apparent that individualism leads to economic disorder and social disharmony. The attention of the economist was, therefore, focussed more and more on the solution of the problems created by individualism and suggesting that the government should adopt a policy of controls in a variety of ways. The neo-classical school closely followed the classical school as far as the pursuit of materialism was concerned, but emphasised the limitations of the policy of *laissez faire.* Pigou, realising that there may be a divergence between individual net product and social net product, studied the fundamental problem of economic action and made a systematic enquiry into all cases where public authority may be justified in intervening.

The doctrine of self-interest, the principle of utility maximisation or the later Hicksian system of 'want satisfaction' all leading to the pursuit of materialism, make a basic assumption of perfect competition to exist in the market. However, as time passed, it became increasingly evident that 'impurities' and 'imperfections' make the existence of 'pure' competition an impossibility. In reality, there is 'monopolistic competition' or 'imperfect competition' that prevails in the market. Chamberlin's thought pointed to 'wastes of monopolistic competition' due to product differentiation, selling and advertisement costs. John Robinson took notice of the 'exploitation' and discriminatory prices by individual firms. Government regulation and control was, therefore, seen as desirable to meet the problems arising out of the imperfections of the market.

In the early twentieth century when the great depression shook the foundation of capitalism, J.M. Keynes appeared on the scene and exposed the shortcomings of what he called the 'individualistic decadent capitalism'. Savings and investments are unconnected activities, the interests of the savers and investors may not coincide because they have different motivations. In an advanced capitalistic economy, a gap between aggregate income and aggregate consumer spending tends to exist, and this is too wide for investment to fill. Consequently, aggregate income will fall and savings will be reduced to restore the balance, but this temporary level of equilibrium is one of less than full employment. Keynes suggested intervention by the state in order to restore and maintain a desirable level of income and employment in the economy. He considered it a 'duty' of the State to order the current volume of investment.[43] Stagnation could be removed by lower interest rates, devaluation, and socialisation of demand. Fiscal and monetary policies of the government could be used to stimulate income and employment.

More Consumption for More Wealth

Consumption is the constituent of effective demand alongwith investment. Keynes, therefore, thought of consumption as an element of prime importance in his economic system and advocated the increase of consumption in all possible ways. He suggested redistributive measures for increasing the propensity to consume. "Measures for the redistribution of incomes in a way likely to raise the propensity to consume may positively be favourable to the growth of capital".[44] Consumption is the cause of demand and demand leads to production; Keynes, therefore, put consumption before production and concluded, "In contemporary conditions the growth of wealth, so far from being dependent on the abstinence of the rich as is commonly supposed is more likely to be impeded by it".[45] In his obsession with the growth of wealth, Keynes was even prepared to adopt means which he considered 'foul'. As he suggests in the *Economic Possibilities for Our Grand Children*, "For at least one hundred years we must pretend to ourselves and to every one that fair is foul and foul is fair; for foul is useful and fair is not. Avarice and usury and precaution must be our gods for a little longer still. For only they can lead us out of the tunnel of economic necessity into daylight".[46]

The Marxian Approach

Karl Marx saw inherent contradictions in the capitalistic economic system. Marx deeply studied the laws of motion of the capitalist society and predicted the doom of capitalism on the basis of his philosophy of dialectical materialism. He was greatly influenced by Hegelian idea of dialectical change being embedded in human affairs. Marx was also influenced by Darwin's views on evolution that in the struggle for existence, 'natural selection' secures the 'survival of the fittest'.

Marx applied the Hegelian idea of dialectics to economic life and gave a materialistic interpretation of history. According to the Marxian philosophy, all the social institutions and the general character of the social and political processes of life are determined and conditioned by economic circumstances, especially the modes of production. As the modes of production change due to development in techniques, inventions and discoveries, there is need for the social institutions to change and adapt themselves accordingly. The institutions, however, have a tendency to become fixed and, therefore, have to be shaken off by revolution. Marx thus held that ultimately all history is the product of materialistic forces.

There is a sharp antagonism between the interests of the bourgeoisie and the proletariat in the capitalistic system and so Marx had predicted that the inherent contradictions in the system would lead us into a completely different system of social and economic relations. The change is inevitable and, therefore, we must understand and cooperate with the circumstances to hasten the process of change. The capitalists are profit hungry people and go on accumulating capital by exploiting the workers. Being the owners of the means of production, the capitalists pay the workers only their subsistence value, i.e., socially necessary labour, and force them to work for the longest possible hours in order to create surplus value.[47] Competition in the market, forces a rise in the wages. The capitalists try to overcome the situation by introducing technological advancement and labour-saving devices, thus changing the organic composition of capital. This leads to displacement of labour and creation of an industrial reserve army. The rate of profits starts falling since it is labour only which creates surplus value. The process goes on and on and the ratio of living labour to total output keeps on falling still further. Ultimately consumption is affected; there is overproduction since the small purchasing power with the workers is unable to take off the market whatever has been produced. A capitalist crisis ensues and smaller firms, therefore, are driven out of business. After some time, the surplus value reappears, competition takes place, technological improvements are introduced and the same drama is once again repeated leading to another crisis. The bigger firms keep on absorbing the smaller firms as crisis after crisis takes place, the industrial reserve army of workers keeps on expanding, the falling rate of profits continues and the consumption goes on dwindling. Ultimately the revolution takes place, the workers throw off the big giants and seize the means of production. The death knell of the capitalist private property sounds. The expropriaters are expropriated.

Violence is embedded in the Marxian system of thought. One force is to be coerced or completely destroyed by the other in order to achieve certain materialistic ends. There is no possibility of the two opposite forces understanding each other and living in peace and harmony. To begin with, the force of the workers overthrows the force of the capitalists, by using violent means. According to the Communist Manifesto, "They openly declare that their ends can be attained only by the forcible overthrow of all existing social relations. Let the ruling classes tremble at a Communist revolution. The proletarians have nothing to lose but their chains. They have a world to win".[48] Now, there is no reason to assume that the winners having lost their chains would be in any way qualitatively better than the ones they have destroyed and that their victory would put an end to the history of the class struggle. As Karl Marx had himself realised, "This too will pass away". The reference to a wry joke that went round in Poland and Czechoslovakia, by Paul Samuelson, in 'Economics' very aptly sums up the situation, "under capitalism, it's a case of man exploiting man. Under socialism, it's a case of *vice versa*".[49] Contradictions would, therefore, reappear and the same process of one force destroying the other would be repeated.

According to the non-Marxists, man is functioning under the force of 'self-interest', whereas according to the Marxists, man has to function under the control of the State. Both the schools of thought thus hold a mechanistic concept of man. After the revolution, the control over the means of production is vested with the State. The individual is left with little liberty and the decisions regarding production, consumption and distribution are taken by the central authority according to its own interest. At the international level, however, the behaviour of the Communist State is just like that of the individual pursuing his self-interest in a competitive market. The same fragmentary world-view is adopted. The only change that is introduced is that now 'group interest' instead of the individual 'self-interest' is being pursued; the group being a part of the whole. The goal of undifferentiated growth or unlimited material progress remains the same. The dedication for technological advancement is again the same as under capitalism due to competition in the world market. Exploitation of nature and the poor countries goes on unabated for the material progress of the State.

A philosophical analysis of the various schools of economic thought makes it obvious that the basic paradigm underlying economics is the same. There is a universal adherence to the fragmentary world-view. Man is taken to be a mechanistic material being having unlimited wants. More and more goods and services are required for the 'betterment', 'happiness' or 'well-being' of man and society. The purpose of economics is the augmentation of wealth, increase of material welfare or increase in the annual flow of goods and services now as well as in future. The performance of an economy is to be judged by the rate of growth of GNP. There are inherent contradictions in the pursuit of materialism as man gets placed against man, society and nature. It is believed that the economic problems can be solved by the State intervention and a policy of controls on man's economic activities. In recent years, there has been a tremendous increase in the State activities to curb individual economic freedom and promote social welfare. Paradoxically, the economic problems have multiplied and become more and more complex. Modern economics looks for a solution to the economic problems within the existing framework of economics instead of looking at the meta-economic factors or exploring its basic philosophical foundations.

NOTES

1. Bertrand Russel, *History of Western Philosophy*, London, George Allen & Unwin Ltd., 1957, p. 143.
2. Ibid., p. 152.
3. *The Greatest is Love*, The Living New Testament, South Holland, The World Home Bible League, 1967, p. 4.
4. *The Republic of Plato*, London, J.M. Dent & Sons Ltd., 1950, pp. 146-154.

5. Quoted in James Bonar, *Philosophy and Political Economy,* 2nd impression, London, George Allen & Unwin Ltd., 1967, p. 52.
6. Quoted in Lewis H. Haney, *History of Economic Thought,* New York, The Macmillan Company, 1964, p. 71.
7. *The Greatest Is Love,* op. cit., p. 7.
8. *The Republic of Plato,* op. cit., p. 106.
9. Haney, op. cit., p. 71.
10. Quoted in Fritjof Capra, *The Turning Point,* London, Fontana Paper backs, 1983, p. 42.
11. Bertrand Russel, *History of Western Philosophy,* op. cit., pp. 585-586.
12. Bertrand Russel, ibid., p. 590.
13. Quoted in Fritjof Capra, *The Turning Point,* op. cit., p. 47.
14. Ibid., p. 49.
15. Ibid., p. 51.
16. James Bonar, *Philosophy and Political Economy,* op. cit., p. 378.
17. Lewis H. Haney, *History of Economic Thought,* op. cit., p. 8.
18. Quoted in Bertrand Russel, *History of Western Philosophy,* p. 637.
19. Mark A. Lutz & Kenneth Lux, *The Challenge of Humanistic Economics,* California, The Benjamin/Cummings Publicity Company, 1979, p. 7.
20. James Bonar, *Philosophy and Political Economy,* op. cit., p. 78.
21. Ramashray Roy, *Gandhi Soundings in Political Philosophy,* Delhi, Chanakya Publication, 1984, p. 6.
22. Quoted in Adam Smith, *The Wealth of Nations,* New York, 1937, p. liii (The Modern Library, Random House, Inc.).
23. James Bonar, *Philosophy and Political Economy,* op. cit., p. 382.
24. Charles Darwin, *The Origin of Species,* 6th ed., New York, The New American Library, 1872, pp. 73-75, 87-88.
25. Lewis H. Haney, *History of Economic Thought,* op. cit., p. 15.
26. Ibid., p. 207.
27. Adam Smith, *The Wealth of Nations,* op. cit., p. 324.
28. Ibid., p. 30.
29. Lewis H. Haney, *History of Economic Thought,* op. cit., p. 8.
30. Quoted in Ramashray Roy, *Gandhi Soundings in Political Philosophy,* op. cit. p. 5.
31. Adam Smith, *The Wealth of Nations,* op. cit., p. lix.
32. Ibid., p. 30.
33. Ibid., p. 14.
34. Quoted in Lewis H. Haney, *History of Economic Thought,* op. cit., p. 212.
35. Adam Smith, *The Wealth of Nations,* op. cit., p. 508.
36. Robert Heilbroner, *The Worldly Philosophers,* Great Britain, Pelican Books, 1983, p. 55.
37. Lewis H. Haney, *History of Economic Thought,* op. cit., p. 469.
38. Ibid., p. 472.
39. James Bonar, *Philosophy and Political Economy,* op. cit., p. 272.
40. Alfred Marshal, *Principles of Economics,* 8th ed., London, Macmillan and Co. Ltd., 1959, p. 73.
41. Ibid., p. 73.
42. E.F. Schumacher, *Small is Beautiful,* op. cit., p. 40.

43. John Maynard Keynes, *The General Theory of Employment, Interest and Money*, London, Macmillan & Co. Ltd., 1960, p. 320.
44. Ibid., p. 373.
45. Ibid.
46. Quoted in James Bonar, *Philosophy and Political Economy*, op. cit., p. 390.
47. Karl Marx, *Capital*, Vol. 1, Moscow, Foreign Languages Publishing House, pp. 216-217.
48. Karl Marx and Frederick Engels, *Manifesto of the Communist Party, Selected Works*, Vol. 1, Moscow, Foreign Languages Publishing House, 1951, p. 61.
49. Paul Samuelson, *Economics*, Auckland, McGraw-Hill, 1980, p. 798.

3

THE ECONOMIC CRISIS

MODERN ECONOMIC system based upon the fragmentary world-view has given rise to a host of irrepressible and uncontrollable economic problems. The nature and magnitude of these problems is such that they defy all solutions within the framework of economics. These problems affecting man's life at various levels have created a multi-dimensional world economic crisis. The economic tools based on the 'reductionist' principle seem to have become quite ineffective in coming to grips with the modern economic crisis which is of a complex and global nature. The economic forces generated by the paradigm underlying modern economics to make man happy are, as a matter of fact, destroying the happiness of man and are threatening to pull down the very system which they have created.

Depletion of Non-renewable Resources

"Earth provides enough to satisfy every man's need but not for every man's greed",[1] observed Mahatma Gandhi long ago. The resources of the world are quasi-insufficient. They are sufficient to fulfil our needs but insufficient to satisfy our wants. However, the purpose of modern economics is provisioning of more and more goods as man is supposed to be having wants which are ever-increasing and ever-multiplying. The efforts of all the nations in the world are, therefore, concentrated in achieving higher and higher rates of economic growth in order to meet the ever-increasing wants. As a result, the world production is increasing at exponential rates. Production, however, requires not only man-made capital but also natural capital in the form of mineral, soil and fuel resources. The natural resources are generally non-renewable having a fixed mass. Since the world population is increasing and consumption levels are moving up causing a higher and higher resource demand, the depletion of world resources is going on exponentially. It is being increasingly realised now that a dangerous situation of exhausting our fixed resource-base might soon arise, if present economic trends remain unaltered. The Club of Rome in collaboration with the MIT Research Team have stated, "Given present resource consumption rates and the projected increase in these rates, the great majority of the currently important non-renewable resources will be extremely costly 100 years from now".[2] They have further declared, "The above statement remains true regardless of the most optimistic assumptions about undiscovered reserves, technological advances, substitution or recycling, as long as the demand for resources continues to grow exponentially".[3]

The following figures regarding ten important non-renewable natural resources of the world may be quoted from 'The Limits to Growth', to show their future situation:

Non-Renewable Natural Resources[4]

Resource	Known Global Resource[a]	Static Index (yrs.)[b]	Projected Rate of Growth (% per year)[a]	Exponential Index (yrs.)[c]	Exponential Index calculated using 5 times known Resources (years)[d]
Aluminum	1.17×10^9 tons	100	6.4	31	55
Coal	5×10^{12} tons	2300	4.1	111	150
Copper	308×10^6 tons	36	4.5	21	48
Iron	1×10^{11} tons	240	1.8	93	173
Lead	91×10^6 tons	26	2.0	21	64
Manganese	8×10^8 tons	97	2.9	46	94
Mercury	3.34×10^6 flasks	13	2.6	13	41
Natural Gas	1.14×10^{15} cu. ft.	38	4.7	22	49
Petroleum	455×10^9 bbls	31	3.9	20	50
Zinc	123×10^6 tons	23	2.9	18	50

a. *Source:* US Bureau of Mines, *Mineral Facts and Problems,* 1970.
b. The number of years known global reserves will last at current global consumption. Calculated by dividing known reserves (column 2) by the current annual consumption (US Bureau of Mines, *Mineral Facts and Problems,* 1970).
c. The number of years known global reserves will last with consumption growing exponentially at the average rate of growth.
d. The number of years that five times known global reserves will last with consumption growing exponentially.

E.F. Schumacher has also made an exploratory calculation regarding the consumption of our fossil fuels. If the rich populations grow at the rate of 1.25 per cent, and the poor at the rate of 2.5 per cent a year, world population would grow to about 6900 million by A.D. 2000. If at the same time, the fuel consumption per head of the 'rich' population grows by 2.25 per cent, while that of the 'poor' grows by 4.5 per cent a year, the world fuel consumption would grow from 5.5. milliard tons c.e. in 1966 to 23.2 milliard in the year 2000 — an increase by a factor of more than four. The world fuel consumption at these consumption rates would have used 425,000 million tons c.e. by the year 2000. According to Schumacher, in the light of our present knowledge of fossil fuel reserves, this is an implausible figure, even if we assume that one-quarter or one-third of the world total would come from nuclear-fission.[5]

It is thus clear from the above estimates that the world is threatened with a problem of depleting non-renewable resources. The impact of the depleting world resources has already begun to be felt in the steep rise in the prices of some of the important resources like petroleum, mercury and lead in the recent years. The price of mercury for example has gone up 500 per cent in the last 20 years and that of lead has increased by 300 per cent in the last 30 years.[6]

The Problem of Ecology

Man is a part of an ecosystem comprising of the earth, air, water, plants and animals, having natural ecological processes. There is inter-connectedness and inter-dependence among the various constituents of the ecosphere. No human activity is possible without the support of the environment and reciprocally, the environment does not remain unaffected by human activity. Regarding the constitution of our environment, the famous environmentalist Barry Commoner has said, "The environment makes up a huge, enormously complex living machine that forms a thin dynamic lawyer on the earth's surface and every human activity depends on the integrity and proper functioning of the machine".[7] The ecosystem consisting of multiple interconnected parts which act and react upon one another must not be disturbed in order to facilitate a smooth functioning of life, economic as well as non-economic. As exemplified by Barry Commoner, "Without the photosynthetic activity of green plants, there would be no oxygen for our engines, smelters and furnaces, let alone support for human and animal life. Without the action of the plants, animals and micro-organisms that live in them, we could have no pure water in our lakes and rivers. Without the biological processes that have gone on in the soil for thousands of years, we would neither have food crops, oil nor coal".[8]

The production of goods needs not only man-made capital but also 'biological capital' represented by a properly balanced ecosphere. As a matter of fact, the ecosphere is the background against which the entire game of our economic activities takes place. The various constituents of the ecosphere must operate in a state of balance in order to provide the necessary biological capital for the economic activities. However, modern industrial processes to produce more and more wealth create a disturbance in the operation of the ecological forces of nature. As a result, the natural cycles get disordered and our soil, air and water become polluted. The environmental pollution not only creates the problem of externalities for the economist but also poses the question of the very survival of human race.

The ecological balance is self-renewable within certain limits. To a certain extent the natural ecological system can absorb the effluents of human activity and replenish and regenerate itself. E.F. Schumacher has referred to this absorbing capacity of the ecosystem as the 'tolerance margins'[9] which the benign nature always provides. There is thus an upper limit to the exploitation of our biological capital. If the 'tolerance margins' of nature are crossed and effluents are released on a scale without any limits, the natural absorbtive mechanisms may break down destroying the ecological balance and creating intolerable levels of pollution. As Barry Commoner has pointed out, "The total rate of exploitation of the earth's ecosystem has some upper limit, which reflects the intrinsic limit of the ecosystem's turnover rate. If this rate is exceeded the system is eventually driven to collapse".[10] A limit to the rate of turnover of the ecosystem automatically means that there has to be a limit to the use of man-made capital also if the ecosystem which is the base of all production is not to be destroyed. As suggested by Gandhiji, according to the principle of an economy of permanence, we should not borrow from nature what cannot be returned to her. Therefore, there must be limits to production, industrialisation and use of technology. Barry Commoner says, "there must be some limit to the growth of total capital, and the productive system must eventually reach a 'no growth' condition at least with respect to the accumulation of capital goods designed to exploit the ecosystem, and the products which they yield".[11]

Nature wills that there should be a limit to the intrusion of man and, therefore, a limit to the production of goods. However, modern economic system is concerned with the provisioning of unlimited goods for the satisfaction of multiple human wants. Man is a small, but an integral part of the whole, the ecosystem. Yet due to the acceptance of the fragmentary world-view, he looks upon the ecosystem as an object of exploitation instead of being in cooperation and acting in tune with it. Consequently, a clash between man's efforts to achieve unlimited production and the upper limit of the ecosystem's rate of turnover becomes inevitable. The imbalance between what man wants to have and what nature is willing to give results in the environmental crisis.

The quest for the maximisation of gains leads to innovations, technological progress and large-scale industrialisation. The obsession with undifferentiated economic growth and the problem of depleting resources leads to the adoption of technologies which are counter-ecological, displacing those which are simple and less destructive. No doubt, modern agriculture and manufacturing industries have become highly productive and efficient by the adoption of recent advanced technologies, but they are consuming our environmental capital at an alarming rate. A greater part of the sharp increase in pollution levels is due not so much to the growth of population or affluence as to changes in productive technology. The increase in population accounts for 12 to 20 per cent of the various increases in total pollutant output since 1946. The affluence factor (i.e., amount of economic good per capita) accounts for 1 to 5 per cent of the total increase in pollutant output. The technology factor, that is, the increased output of pollutants per unit production resulting from the introduction of new productive technologies since 1946 accounts for 80 to 85 per cent of the total output of pollutants.[12] Putting the blame squarely on modern technology for degradation of our environment, Vance Hartke Commoner says, "A runaway technology, whose only law is profit, has for years poisoned our air, ravaged our soil, stripped our forests bare and corrupted our water resources".[13]

The ecosystem is destabilised due to the disruption of three major mechanisms of nature, i.e., disruption of essential chemical cycles, disruption of energy flow, and disruption of the diversity of species and food webs. Modern industrial process and technological progress have resulted in an environmental crisis in the world due to the disturbances of all these three basic mechanisms by which the ecosystem maintains itself.

Modern agricultural and industrial processes have meant an incursion upon our environment beyond tolerable limits and have resulted in breaking down of the self-purifying cycles of air, water and soil due to the disruption of the above-mentioned natural mechanisms. Air pollution has become a big health hazard in modern times. In 1952, smog in London killed 4,000 people in 5 days. These days, the air contains pollutants like sulphurdioxide, nitrogen oxide, hydrocarbons, dust originating from furnace ash, industrial operations and the wearing down of motor tyres and asphalt paving by traffic; asbestos' particles, mercury vapour from industrial operations and a variety of organic compounds released into the air by combustion and chemical industrial process. Barry Commoner has calculated that modern urban air contains more than 39 pollutants not found in 'natural air'.[14]

The toxic metals, lead and mercury are released into the waterways and into the atmosphere from automobiles, incinerators, industrial processes and agricultural pesticides. In parts of our hydrosphere, especially the deeper waters, oxygen concentration has become almost zero and no form of aquatic life can be supported there. Our rivers and ponds are being polluted by indiscrete dumping of sewage and industrial waste into them. The soil system has been overdriven damaging the self-renewable capacity of the soil and therefore leading to soil deterioration. Increasing use of the pesticides is gradually reducing the efficiency of the soil to rejuvenate itself and is further posing a big threat to wildlife and man. Deforestation is another disastrous activity which has created ecological imbalance leading to disturbance in the water cycle resulting in crop failure, unprecedented floods and reduced efficiency of the soil.

Development of nuclear power for war time as well as for peaceful purposes in order to meet the threat of depleting resources and make recycling and substitution possible is another source responsible for contaminating the environment to dangerous levels. Atomic radiation does not remain localised, it has a global impact affecting every plant, animal and human-being on this earth. Radioactive pollutants are carried to the different parts of the earth through the agents of wind, rain and snow. Crops and grass absorb them and further pass on to animals and men. Radiation results in cancer, genetic defects, general life-shortening and many other diseases of modern times.

Modern economic activities are resulting in continued energy growth in the environment and threatening irreversible climatic changes. In the opinion of Stephen Schneider, Deputy Head of the National Centre for Atmospheric Research, this will "cause climatic changes that could be both global and irreversible" after the year 2000.[15] Thus, manmade heat is steadily being added to the solar energy received from the Sun. According to Robert Heilbroner, "At present energy growth rates, in 150 years manmade heat throw off will equal about one per cent of the energy received from the sun. A continuation of these rates for another century would render the planet uninhabitable".[16]

Obsession with unlimited economic abundance leads to war with all its disastrous consequences. As a result of he Gulf War the world environment has already started being adversely affected. Gulf regions are having acidic black rains due to the burning of oil wells. Kashmir Valley is experiencing black snow containing poisonous chemicals such as arsenic, zinc, lead etc. The acidic elements are damaging the forests and polluting the soil, air and water, causing destruction of the eco-system in the valley.

Estimating the cost of environmental degradation is very difficult as it takes various forms and involves qualitative assessment. The environmental costs may appear as damage costs, avoidance costs and abatement costs. Damage costs are the direct costs of pollution itself. Avoidance costs are those incurred by people in attempting to separate themselves from pollution. Transaction costs are the costs of gathering information about pollution. Abatement costs are those incurred in abating pollution. In certain cases, the costs of environmental damage are not quantitatively definable at all. What could be the cost of the damage caused by pollution of the holy Ganges or despoiling of the scenic beauty of the Doon Valley? The costs of the lives lost by atomic radiation, Bhopal, Chernobyl Disaster, and the suffering caused by diseases such as cancer, leukemia and genetic defects is certainly immeasurable.

As man continues with his relentless pursuit of more and more, the environmental costs escalate at an exponential rate. These costs may soon outbid the benefits received by man's economic activities. The use of technology to control pollution leads to further pollution of various kinds. Generally, it is simply a case of trading one pollution problem for another. Moreover, it is not possible to eliminate certain kinds of pollution, such as, thermal pollution and radio-isotopes from nuclear power generation, fertilizer run off an asbestos particles from break linings.

The Collapse

It is obvious that we are on a 'collision course', if dominated by the present paradigm, man continues his endless race towards more and more. Under the present circumstances, the clash between limits of nature and unlimited desires of man may soon lead to the collapse of the very industrial system and may even endanger human survival. In recent years, there has been an awakened consciousness regarding the problems of undifferentiated growth and many famous economists, environmentalists and intellectuals in other fields are giving strong warnings against the future shape of things. Robert L. Heilbroner, in *Business Civilisation in Decline*, feels that industrial growth is an exponential process — a process that proceeds like a snowball, generating continuously increasing quantities of wastes, simply to maintain a constant pace of expansion. No social processes of an exponential character are capable of indefinite continuance. Sooner or later all such processes must overload their environment, consuming all its nutrients or poisoning it by waste products associated with growth.[17] Heilbroner has therefore concluded, "From the pollution side, then as well as from that of resource availability, we have some general empirical findings that make an estimate of 100 years a plausible approximation of the time span within which growth must come to a halt".[18] E.F. Schumacher who seriously questions the idea of unlimited economic growth leading to more and more until everybody is saturated with wealth declares, "economic growth, which viewed from the point of view of economics, physics, chemistry and technology, has no discernible limit must necessarily run into decisive bottle-necks when viewed from the point of view of the environmental sciences. An attitude to life which seeks fulfilment in the single-minded pursuit of wealth — in short, materialism — does not fit into this world, because it contains within itself no limiting principle, while the environment in which it is placed is strictly limited".[19]

Barry Commoner in his famous book, *The Closing Circle*, expresses his serious concern about our present economic system being fast driven to bankruptcy, "Since the usefulness of conventional capital depends on the existence of the biological capital — the ecosystem — when the latter is destroyed, the usefulness of the former is also destroyed. Thus, despite its apparent prosperity, in reality the system is being driven into bankruptcy. Environmental degradation represents a crucial, potentially fatal, hidden factor in the operation of the economic system".[20] Regarding the inherent contradictions present in our system, he further comments wryly, "We are in an environmental crisis because the means by which we use the ecosphere to produce wealth are destructive of the ecosphere itself. The present system of production is self-destructive; the present course of human civilisation is suicidal".[21]

Hazel Henderson talking in terms of costs and benefits, says, "The Cartesian world-view leads us to ignore the link between private profits and the mounting public costs they engender".[22] Due to the rising environmental and social costs of growth, we are soon likely to reach the 'entropy state' which she explains as "a society at the state when complexity and interdependence have reached the point where the transaction costs that are generated equal or exceed the society's productive capabilities".[23] The Club of Rome headed by Donella Meadows in collaboration with the MIT Research Team made a deep study of the growth trends in the five basic quantities or levels—population, capital, food, non-renewable resources and pollution. Taking into consideration their interactions and positive feedback loops, with the aid of a computer, using global data, they have concluded that the limits to growth on this planet will be reached sometime within the next one hundred years. The most probable results will be a rather sudden and uncontrollable decline in both population and industrial capacity.[24] The analysis of overshoot and collapse may be summed up as follows:

(1) Expanding industrial output requires an enormous input of resources, ultimately leading to the depletion of a large fraction of the resource reserves available.
(2) As the resource reserves are depleted, the resource prices rise high and, therefore, more and more industrial expenditure goes for obtaining the resources leaving less and less to be invested for future growth.
(3) Finally investment cannot keep up with depreciation and the industrial base collapses.

(4) In collapsing the industrial sector carries with it the services and agricultural sectors, which have become dependent on industrial sector, using fertilizers, pesticides, hospital laboratories, computers and especially energy for mechanisation.

(5) Population, with the delays inherent in the age structure and the process of social adjustment, keeps rising.

(6) Finally, population is checked by a sharp rise in death rate due to the decreasing food supply and disrupting health services. The writers of *The Limits to Growth* further maintain that advances in technology, programmes of recycling and resource substitution cannot in any case avert the collapse, they can merely delay the process. If these changes are the only ones introduced in the system, growth is ultimately stopped by rising environmental pollution.

Poverty and Hunger

The problem of poverty and hunger in the world is the greatest stigma upon modern economics. The number of the poor and the hungry has been constantly increasing all over the world inspite of all the efforts at rapid economic growth. Moreover, as held by Lutz and Lux, poverty as we know it, is a relatively recent phenomenon; poverty did not exist four hundred years ago. To quote them, "Surprising as it may sound, the modern phenomenon of poverty had its beginning with the Enclosure Movement in England. Previous to that under the stable order of traditional society, poverty pockets as we know them now were almost non-existent".[26]

Modern economic growth backed by high investment and industrialisation has been unable to control the ratio of poverty. According to the ILO report, *Employment, Growth and Basic Needs in 1972*, some 1,200 million people in the developing market economies (67% of their population) were seriously poor, and 700 million (39%) were 'destitutes' and suffering from severe malnutrition. The two poverty lines were based respectively on the average earnings of unskilled labour in large scale manufacturing enterprises in India and on the equivalent of one rupee per person per day in Indian terms. The details of the number of the poor in developing economies are given as follows:

Estimated number of people in developing market economics living in poverty, 1972[27]

Region	Total population	Seriously poor	Destitutes	Seriously poor	Destitutes
	(Million of People)			(Percentage of Population)	
Asia	1,196	853	499	71	42
Africa	345	239	134	69	39
Latin America	274	118	73	43	27
Total* :	1,815	1,210	706	67	39

* Excluding developing countries in Europe and Oceania, with a total population of about 25 million.

Increase in Poverty- 1963-72[28]

(Figures in millions of persons)

Region	Total Population	Seriously Poor	Destitutes
Asia	195	92	34
Africa	68	26	5
Latin America	62	1	4
Total* :	325	119	43

* Excluding developing countries in Europe and Oceania, with a total population of about 25 million.

According to the World Development Report (1990), there are one billion people in the world who are poor. In India, several attempts have been made to estimate the total number of poor people, as well as to study the change in them over the years. Dr. Raj Krishna maintains that in the past, the growth of average income has left the poverty ratios unchanged. Using figures from *Measurement of Poverty in India* by K.L. Datta, he concludes, "The rural poverty ratio was statistically stable around 58.2 per cent and the total poverty ratio around 56.6 per cent while income per capita growing at the low average of 1 per cent a year during 1960-61/1973-74".[29] As reported by Planning Commission, 1990, there were 200 million people who were below the poverty line in India. The actual figures may be much above this estimate. According to the estimates of B.S. Minhas, L.R. Jain and S.D. Tendulkar, the current incidence of poverty in India is 44.8 per cent and 36.5 per cent in rural and urban areas respectively.

The suffering caused by hunger and poverty is unmeasureable. Cold statistics speak little about this part and, therefore, they are quite inadequate in measuring the incidence of the problem of poverty. According to Lutz and Lux, "One person's economic deprivation and suffering is equal to the suffering of an infinity of persons. If a million people suffer, each is suffering as an individual. The Arithmetic of suffering, therefore, does not respect the adding machine".[30] Deeply moved by the suffering of the poor and the hungry, Gandhiji had felt that eradication of poverty must be the basic motivational force of economic action of man and society. He said, "I will give you a talisman. Whenever you are in doubt, or when the self becomes too much with you, apply the following test. Recall the face of the poorest and the weakest man whom you may have seen, and ask yourself, if the step you contemplate is going to be of any use to him. Will he gain anything by it? Will it restore him to a control over his own life and destiny? In other words, will it lead to 'Swaraj' for the hungry and spiritually starving millions? Then you find your doubts and yourself melting away".[31]

Inequalities of Income

The fragmentary world-view divides life and sets one part against the other. In the economic sphere, the paradigm has resulted in sharp inequalities of income and wide disparities at the regional as well as international level. Modern growth model leading to large-scale capital intensive, technologically advanced methods of production is responsible for the increasing level of concentration of economic power and has led to the accentuation of inequalities of income and further widening of the gulf between the rich and the poor.

According to the ILO Estimates, benefits of growth and in particular opportunities for productive employment, have mainly gone to a very small part of the total population in developing countries. The richest 10 per cent of households in most developing countries typically receive about 40 per cent of the personal income, whereas the poorest 40 per cent receive 15 per cent or less, and the bottom 20 per cent receive about 5 per cent. Income distribution is highly unequal not only at the national but also at the international level. In 1972, the industrial market economy countries, with only 17 per cent of the world population, accounted for 67 per cent of total world output. At the other extreme, 26 per cent of the world's population lived in countries whose total output accounted for under 3 per cent of the world total. If China were included, the data suggests that 47 per cent of the population received less than 7 per cent of the world's income. The report further maintains that in absolute terms differentials are widening rapidly. This is because, say, an annual growth rate of 2 per cent per head in a very rich country such as Sweden or the United States is virtually equal to the total product per head of a very poor country. Relatively also, the inequality has continued to increase. The most dramatic increase in international inequality, however, is within the group of developing countries. There has been a very noticeable tendency in recent years for the poorest of the developing countries to grow less rapidly than the less poor.[32]

In developed economies also, there is high degree of concentration of income and wealth. Paul Samuelson has given a very interesting graphic analogy regarding the skewed distribution of income in the United States. "If we made today an income pyramid out of a child's blocks, with each layer portraying $ 1000 of income, the peak would be far higher than the Eiffel Tower, but almost all of us would be within a yard of the ground".[33]

It is becoming more and more evident these days that growth does not trickle down to the poor on its own in the presumed Keynesian manner. The benefit of growth and development mostly go to the richer sections of the society. According to the estimates given by Dandekar and Rath in their work *Poverty in India*, the overall increase in per capita consumption in India from 1960-61 to 1967-68 was 3.8 per cent. However, even these meagre gains were shared very unequally. The consumption of the upper 40 per cent of the urban population rose by atleast 4.8 per cent and that of the upper 40 per cent of the rural population by 4.4 per cent. Other sections of the population, both urban and rural, showed much smaller increases in their per capita consumption. The per capita consumption of the poorest 5 per cent in the rural area and the bottom 40 per cent in the urban area actually declined. The situation is more serious in urban area, where the per capita consumption of the poorest 10 per cent actually slumped by as much as 15 to 20 per cent.[34] Thus, we see that growth and development is actually accentuating inequalities of income.

Inequalities of income and wealth are the source of many social and economic evils. They lead to the emergence of social tensions and sharpening of class conflicts. Strictly in economic terms, gross inequalities of income adversely affect production and investment and lead to the malallocation of resources. Man suffers not only from absolute poverty but also from relative poverty created by inequalities of income. Growth itself obstructs the availability of certain comforts to every one. Moreover, certain goods having a 'positional' character can't be made available to all the people, even if there is a general rise in every one's income levels. For example, every one can't get a home by the sea-shore, even if every one is proportionately much better off. In terms of relative standing, one is in the same position and, therefore, the frustration of not being able to attain a particular social status continues.

Exploitation

Exploitation of the poor by the rich, labour by capital, consumer by producer, village by city are the common features of an economy wedded to the goal of more and more. Condemning the exploitative character of modern economics, Gandhiji had said, "An economics that inculcates Mammon worship, and enables the strong to amass wealth at the expense of the weak is a false and dismal science. It spells death".[35] At the international level, the pursuit of material self-interest has led to the exploitation of the third world countries by the developed countries of for the sake of markets, raw materials and scarce natural resources. The advanced economies which are able to sell their products at competitive prices advertise their products, raise the expectations of the consumers in the poor countries and allure them into buying them. In exchange for these products which are quite unsuitable for the under-developed economies, the developed economies obtain raw materials and scarce resources by offering them highly unfavourable terms of trade. As Hazel Henderson has noted, "Rather than concentrating on increasing self-sufficiency, poor countries, sucked into the whirlpool of world trade, often act in their own worst interest by selling their protein and raising cash crops to exchange for inflation ridden foreign currencies".[36] In the name of technology-transfer, the under-developed countries are dumped with obsolete, harmful technologies and products. Technology transfer generally favours the rich in an under-developed country, and leads to the accentuation of the already existing inequalities of income. The lure of high standards of living in the economically advanced countries drains the educated, the talented and the enterprising out of the poor countries. Bereft of capital resources and talents, the under-developed economies remain entrapped in a low-level equilibrium.

Unemployment

Labour is looked upon simply as an item of cost in modern economics. The producer has to minimise the costs in order to maximise his profits. Machinery, therefore, comes in displacing labour and creating unemployment. Competition amongst the producers leads to technological progress and concentration of capital. Unemployment, therefore, keeps on rising with each step in technological advancement. The problem of unemployment is closely linked with poverty. As a matter of fact, technological advancement, concentration of economic power, inequalities of income, unemployment, poverty and rising population are all interacting factors.

Statistical data regarding unemployment make it sufficiently evident that unemployment has been continuously rising both in the under-developed as well as developed economies inspite of all the efforts at planning, growth and development. The following table shows the rising rate of unemployment in seven countries.

Unemployment in Seven Countries, 1959-76[37]

(Average annual rate according to U.S. definitions)

Year	United States	Australia	Canada	France	West Germany	Great Britain	Sweden
1966	3.8	1.5	3.6	1.8	0.3	2.4	1.6
1967	3.8	1.6	4.1	2.3	1.0	3.8	2.1
1968	3.6	1.5	4.8	2.7	1.2	3.7	2.2
1969	3.5	1.5	4.7	2.1	0.8	3.7	1.9
1970	4.9	1.4	5.7	2.8	0.8	3.7	1.5
1971	5.9	1.6	6.2	3.0	0.8	3.9	2.6
1972	5.6	2.2	6.2	3.0	0.8	4.2	2.7
1973	4.9	1.9	5.6	2.9	0.8	3.2	2.5
1974	5.6	2.3	5.4	3.9	1.7	3.2	2.0
1975	8.5	4.4	6.9	4.3	3.8	4.7	1.6
1976	7.7	4.4	7.1	4.6	3.8	6.4	1.6

Source: Bureau of Labour Statistics.

According to the ILO Estimates, about 5 per cent of the labour force in developing markets economies is openly unemployed. About 36 per cent of the labour force is under-employed, the proportion being less in urban and more in rural areas. About 80 per cent of the total unemployed and under-employed are rural. The following table shows the figures regarding unemployment and under-employment in developing countries.

Preliminary Estimates of unemployment and under-employment in developing countries by region, 1975[38]

(*in millions*)

Region	Unemployment[1]		Underemployment[2]		Total	
	Total Nos.	% age	Total Nos.	% age	Nos.	% age
Asia[3]	18	3.9	168	36.4	186	40.3
Africa	10	7.1	53	37.9	63	45.0
Latin America	5	5.1	28	29.9	33	34.0
Oceania	—	—	1	49.0	1	49.0
Total :	33	4.7	250	35.7	283	40.4

Source: ILO Bureau of Statistics.

1. Defined as "persons without a job and seeking for work".
2. Defined as "persons who are in employment of less than normal duration and who are seeking or would accept additional work".
3. Excluding China and other Asian Centrally planned countries.

Employment is not only a source of livelihood, it also acts as a means to realise one's latent faculties and thus provides man an opportunity for creativity and self-actualisation. Unemployment is a loss both to the individual and the society. Moreover, frustration resulting from the state of unemployment breeds many other socio-economic problems.

Stagflation and Instability

Inflation accompanied by unemployment known as stagflation has become a standing feature of all the industrial economies committed to the path of undifferentiated economic growth. The presumption that there is a trade-off between inflation and unemployment is proving to be unrealistic. Recent years have witnessed a continuous rise in both the rates of inflation as well as unemployment. Unlimited industrialisation accompanied by unhindered technological advancement in order to achieve ever-rising levels of production results in both unemployment and inflation. Unemployment occurs due to the technological progress and industrialisation. Prices start rising due to the mounting environmental and social costs and depleting non-renewable resources. These costs which are initially externalised by the producer ultimately start making their impact upon the price level. The existing inequalities of income and wealth create social tensions and therefore the non-capitalist sections of the economy always keep making efforts to push up the levels of their incomes by creating pressure on the Government and the capitalist class. A gradual rise in the money incomes of the non-capitalist class also adds to the problem of inflation and unemployment. In under-developed economies, increased investment alongwith technologically advanced methods of production leads to inflation and further adds to the problem of unemployment due to the presence of various bottlenecks and lags, lack of capital and necessary infrastructure as well as lack of effective demand.

According to the 'World Development Report, 1984', the world is caught up in a vicious spiral of labour market rigidities, inflation, macroeconomic instability and slow growth. The under-developed countries are in turn affected by what happens in the developed countries.

Throwing light on the factors responsible for the phenomenon, the report says, "Two policy-induced developments deserve particular attention: first, the increasing rigidity of the labour market and the resulting strong upward pressure on real wages; and second, the growth and pattern of public spending, taxation and fiscal deficits. The links between these are at the root of the problem of inflation, unemployment and slow growth. The oil price rises of 1973-74 and 1979-80 aggravated these difficulties and required adjustment which the industrial economies found difficult to make efficiently".[39]

Dehumanisation

Besides problems at the physical material level involving environmental pollution and depletion of resources, socio-economic problems of poverty, inequalities of income, exploitation and unemployment, economic problems of stagflation and instability, adherence to the fragmentary paradigm has led to the problems of alienation of man leading to moral degradation and dehumanisation. As Schumacher has observed, "Our current methods of production are already eating into the very substance of industrial man".[40] As a result, in spite of all our scientific achievements and so-called economic growth and better standards of living, peace and happiness has eluded man. The rate of crime, corruption, drug-addiction, vandalism, mental breakdown, profound social, political, economic discontentment and rebellion and the constant haunting fear of a nuclear holocast are some of the symptoms expressing deep frustration and unhappiness of modern man.

Economics of more and more alientes man from his true self the spirit, and obstructs growth into the dimension of love which is expressed in selflessness, cooperation and harmony of relationships. Materialism requires systematic cultivation of greed and envy, pursuit of self-interest. The greed for wealth leads to all sorts of crime and corruption. Man becomes desensitised and remains callously indifferent even in the midst of the problems of poverty, hunger and unemployment of the fellow-beings. As economic progress takes place, moral progress is retarded leading to the qualitative deterioration of human spirit and thus alienation of man from the true self. Criticising modern economic system, Gandhiji wrote in *Hind Swaraj*, "We shall keep our money at the price of our blood because our very moral being will be sapped".[41] The division of society into the classes of the exploiter and the exploited due to the pursuit of materialism involves moral degradation for both. According to Gandhiji, it "involves tyranny, vanity, pride, greed, selfishness, ruthless competition on one side, loss of liberty, insecurity, fears, loss of self-reliance and of independence, degradation, poverty, loss of dignity and self-respect, on the other".[42]

As industrialisation proceeds, man gets increasingly cut off from nature. In fact, nature is ruthlessly destroyed as it is looked upon as an object of exploitation. As urbanisation takes place with technological and industrial advancement, man gets alienated from nature, becomes a victim of congested and polluted surroundings and is deprived of the joys which nature bestows upon him without any cost.

The technological and institutional growth of our economic system leads to alienation from work. Due to the giant size of the organisations, complicated methods of production and technology, the common worker is reduced to the level of a mere cog in the wheel. He just has to perform certain mechanical operation without any understanding of the whole and, therefore, without any attachment to the work, and job satisfaction. Modern economic system thus reduces man to a small part to be used in the big economic machinery. Man is denied freedom for self-expression and is deprived of the opportunity for self-actualisation and creativity. Work therefore becomes a soulless, meaningless, joyless, mechanical activity.

The fragmentary paradigm underlying modern economics has thus led to problems not only at the economic level but also at the environmental, political, social and human levels. The economic problems generated by the pursuit of materialism has become multi-faceted entailing depletion of resources, environmental pollution, ecological imbalance, poverty and hunger, inequalities of income, unemployment, inflation, monetary and economic instability, social and political tension, alienation and dehumanisation. The various problems not only feed upon themselves but also interact upon one another. Moreover, the problems have acquired a global character due to the growth of modern economic institutions and scientific developments. The complexity and the magnitude of these problems is increasing day by day.

Failure of Modern Economic Tools

The traditional fragmentary economic solutions are incapable of tackling the problematique facing mankind. The simple tools of demand and supply and the efforts of the Government at the micro and macro levels are unable to solve the existing problems. The continuously increasing magnitude and the complexity of the world problems bears testimony to this fact. Conventional market mechanism which is essentially based on the pursuit of private interest evidently cannot accommodate the powerful social and environmental costs generated by the process. As described by Lawrence Hines, "For society, however, there are important instances in which the price or cost of a product does not pay for all the unwanted consequences of its production, such as pollution, waste of resources not purchased and aesthetic degradation".[43] The market forces have no in-built mechanism to limit the use of our irreplaceable natural capital. Poverty and inequalities of income and wealth is another problem which lies outside the purview of the market mechanism. The manipulation of aggregate demand and supply does not solve the problems of unemployment. The policy of pumping up economies results on rising rates of inflation and resources depletion. According to Adolph Lowe, in modern times, the forces of demand and supply do not work in the conventional way assuming a fully predictable, self-correcting and self-limiting course, tending toward the establishment of a 'macro-equilibrium' state which represents the production-consumption optimum attainable with the given resources under the prevailing order of income distribution. Explaining the factors responsible for existing disorder, he says, "The progressive substitution of 'satisficing' for 'maximising' behaviour; uncertainty of expectations; prevalence of oligopolies and generally monopolistic manipulations, as a consequence, a narrowing of price and wage fluctuations, rapid technological progress all are responsible for the 'disorder'".[44] The market forces can be of little use in solving our problems of gigantic proportions since modern economy lacks the required responsiveness. Lowe, therefore, believes that it is impossible to construct an economic theory adequate for the present times, due to a lack of that minimum degree of orderliness which is the prerequisite of any scientific generalisation.

In may be added further that the forces of demand and supply have the limitation of treating all work as disutility and disregarding all human costs. The problem of alienation lies outside the scope of price mechanism. As Lutz and Lux have said, "All too often the production of things is enhanced by degrading, fragmenting and alienating labour; in other words, by imposing tremendous human costs that don't enter the calculus of the marketplace".[45] Needless to say that the market forces are, therefore, quite useless in tackling the qualitative problems of human debasement, alienation, lack of freedom and creativity.

The paradoxical situation leads to a tremendous increase in the state activities to provide symptomatic treatment to the problems which can no longer be ignored to promote social and economic welfare curbing individual freedom and entrepreneurial spirit in the process. However, those who have the responsibility to control the situation are the representatives of the very people committed to a fragmentary paradigm, and therefore, try to tackle the situation in parts by providing fragmentary solutions. The fragments are questioned while the basic principle governing life and the other multitude of problems are ignored. The fragmentary solutions prove futile since the problems confronting man are inter-related and inter-connected, tending to be global in nature and touching various levels of life. The contradictions have a tendency to reappear in one form or the other. The Club of Rome therefore, concludes regarding the major problems of the day, "traditional institutions and policies are no longer able to cope with them, not even come to grip with their full content".[46] Explaining why the present crisis can't be resolved, Fritjof Capra has written, "We are trying to apply the concepts of an outmoded world-view — the mechanistic world-view of Cartesian-Newtonian science to a reality that can no longer be understood in terms of these concepts. We live today in a globally inter-connected world in which biological, psychological, social and environmental phenomena are inter-dependent".[47]

A policy of control and re-arrangement of certain factors external to man do not help in creating a harmonious economic order comprising of peace, prosperity and permanence as long as the interest of the 'self' remains fragmented from the interest of the 'non-self'. The controls fail to bridge the gap between what 'is' and what 'ought' to be, because selfishness can always find corrupt means to express itself. Moreover, corruption is sustained, aggravated and perpetuated because the controlling authority comprises of human beings who are themselves prisoners of 'self-interest'.

Dr. Ramashray Roy while interpreting Gandhiji's *Hind Swaraj* says, "the incompatibility that modern civilisation creates between interest and justice overshadows the true purpose of the Parliament and makes it an instrument of protecting and furthering particular interests".[48]

Centrally planned communist economies also do not provide any solution to the world economic problems as the basic paradigm underlying the system remains to be the same. Now the group interest is pursued instead of the individual self-interest. The economy remains committed to the goal of undifferentiated growth or unlimited material progress leading to environmental and social costs, generating the same problems as discussed before. In the Marxian Communist System, a violent struggle takes place to over-threw the bourgeoisie and capture the means of production. Violence which is an outcome of the fragmentary paradigm, is however, not eliminated even after the expropriaters are expropriated. Inspite of complete control on the individual freedom, the roots of violence sprout again and find expression in some form or the other. A new class of the expropriates is born and the high goal when the state whithers away is never realised. Consequently new dialectics arise and the revolution starts taking new shapes. History has once again proved that structures created on the foundations of violence, curbing the freedom of the individual ultimately crumble down. Communism has failed and is fast being wiped out from the world.

NOTES

1. Quoted in E.F. Schumacher, *Small is Beautiful,* New Delhi, Radha Krishna, 1978, p. 29.
2. Donella H. Meadows, *The Limits to Growth,* 2nd ed., New York, Potomac Associates, 1972, p. 75.
3. Ibid.
4. Ibid., pp. 64-66.
5. E.F. Schumacher, *Small is Beautiful,* op. cit., p. 23.
6. Donella H. Meadows, *The Limits to Growth,* op. cit., p. 75.
7. Barry Commoner, *The Closing Circle,* New York, Alfred A. Knopf, 1975, p. 16.
8. Ibid, p. 16.
9. E.F. Schumacher, *Small is Beautiful,* op. cit., p. 15.
10. Barry Commoner, *The Closing Circle,* op. cit., p. 274.
11. Ibid., p. 274.
12. Ibid., p. 176.
13. Quoted Ibid., p. 8.
14. Ibid., p. 76.
15. Quoted in Rober L. Heilbroner, *Business Civilization in Decline,* London, Marion Boyars, 1976, p. 104.
16. Ibid.
17. Ibid., pp. 102-103.
18. Ibid., pp. 105-106.
19. E.F. Schumacher, *Small is Beautiful,* op. cit., p. 25.
20. Barry Commoner, *The Closing Circle,* op. cit., p. 273.
21. Ibid, p. 295.
22. Hazel Henderson, *Creating Alternative Futures,* New York, Berkley Publishing Corporation, 1978, p. 12.
23. Donella H. Meadows, *The Limits to Growth,* op. cit., p. 133.
24. Ibid.
25. Ibid.
26. Mark A. Lutz, and Kenneth Lux, *The Challenge of Humanistic Economics,* California, Benjamin Cummings Publicity Company, 1979, p. 179.
27. International Labour Office, *Employment, Growth and Basic Needs: A One-World Problem,* New York, Praeger, 1977. p. 22.
28. Ibid., p. 23.
29. Raj Krishna, 'Growth, Investment and Poverty in Mid-Term Appraisal of Sixth Plan', *Economic and Political Weekly,* Bombay, November 19, 1983.
30. Mark A. Lutz, and Kenneth Lux, *The Challenge of Humanistic Economics,* op. cit., p. 178.
31. D.C. Tendulkar, *Mahatma,* Vol. VIII, New Delhi, Publications Division, Government of India, 1969, p. 88.
32. International Labour Office, *Employment, Growth and Basic Needs,* op. cit., p. 29.
33. Paul A. Samuelson, *Economics,* 11th ed., Auckland, McGraw-Hill, 1980, p. 80.

34. V.M. Dandekar and N. Rath, *Poverty in India,* Bombay, Indian School of Political Economy Publications, 1971, pp. 25-29.
35. Quoted in V.K.R.V. Rao, *Indian Socialism,* New Delhi, Concept Publishing Company, 1982, p. 63. (*Harijan,* 9-10-1937).
36. Hazel Henderson, *Creating Alternative Futures,* op. cit., pp. 97-98.
37. Mark A. Lutz & Kenneth Lux, *The Challenge of Humanistic Economics,* op. cit., p. 212.
38. International Labour Office, *Employment Growth and Basic Needs,* op. cit., p. 18.
39. The World Bank, *World Development Report,* op. cit., p. 13.
40. E.F. Schumacher, *Small is Beautiful,* op. cit., p. 16.
41. M.K. Gandhi, *Hind Swaraj* or Indian Home Rule, Ahmedabad, Navajivan Publishing House, 1938, p. 94.
42. Ibid., p. 42.
43. Lawrence G. Hines. *Environmental Issues,* New York, Norton and Company, Inc., 1973, p. 93.
44. Adolph Lowe, *Economic Means and Social Ends,* ed. by Robert L. Heilbroner, New Jersey, Prentice Hall, Inc., 1969, p. 171.
45. Mark A. Lutz & Kenneth Lux, *The Challenge of Humanistic Economics,* op. cit., p. 276.
46. Donella H. Meadows, *The Limits to Growth,* op. cit., p. X.
47. Fritjof Capra, *The Turning Point,* London, Flamingo, Fortana paperbacks, 1983, p. XVIII.
48. Ramashray Roy, *Gandhi Sounding,* in Political Philosophy, Delhi, Chanakya Publications, 1984, p. 8.

4

GANDHIAN HOLISTIC APPROACH

GANDHIJI HAD a holistic vision of life. He believed that there is an ultimate unity and wholeness in all that exists, manifested as well as unmanifested. The holistic paradigm led Gandhiji to have a particular concept of the self, society, a purpose of life and certain norms and values to live by. All his ideas and actions, economic as well as non-economic, were the direct outcome of a holistic world-view. It is essential to be clear about Gandhiji's holistic approach in order to understand his economic thought, the principles, policy, analysis or system.

Faith in God

Mahatma Gandhi had an immovable faith in the existence of God. Faith in God was the guiding star of all his actions in any field; life without faith in God was unimaginable for him. "I am surer of His existence than of the fact that you and I are sitting in this room. Then I can also testify that I may live without air and water but not without Him. You may pluckout my eyes, but that cannot kill me. You may chop off my nose, but that will not kill me. But blast my belief in God, and I am dead",[1] he declared. Faith for him is not contradictory to reason but it is the end of reason which leads him to the beginning of faith. "There are subjects where reason cannot take us far and we have to accept things on faith. Faith then does not contradict reason but transcends it. Faith is a kind of sixth sense which works in cases which are without the purview of reason".[2] Gandhiji had deeply studied Eastern and Western philosophies including the *Upanishads*, the *Puranas*, the *Gita*, the *Bible*, the *Quran*, etc. He had learnt a lot from the Indian saints and had been greatly influenced by John Ruskin, Tolstoy and other social thinkers. He had been with Shrimad Rajchandra, a great saint of Gujarat, for sometime to understand the reality of life. It was only after a great intellectual and spiritual churning that he had come to develop; a living faith in the existence of God.

Having been born in a Hindu family, Gandhiji felt a sacred bond with Hinduism. He was greatly inspired by the Hindu religion and felt elated by the music of the Gita and the Ramayana. However, ultimately he worshipped the Truth as was not prepared to accept anything that went against his spiritual and moral understanding. As Romain Rolland writes, "Gandhiji believes in the religion of his people, in Hinduism. But he is not a scholar attached to the punctilious interpretation of texts nor is he a blind believer accepting unquestioningly all the traditions of his religion. His religion must satisfy his reason and correspond to the dictates of his conscience".[3] Gandhiji would not compromise with anything that went down the sieve of his personal understanding of the Truth. "My belief in the Hindu scriptures does not require me to accept every word and every verse as divinely inspired. I decline to be bound by any interpretation, however learned it may be if it is repugnant to reason or moral sense".[4] Moreover, Gandhiji never considered Hindu religion to be the only way to God realisation. In *Hind Swaraj*, he makes it very clear that "Religions are different roads converging to the same point".[5] In another context, he has said very pointedly, "I do not believe in the exclusive divinity of the *Vedas*. I believe the *Bible*, the *Koran* and the *Zend-Avesta* to be as divinely inspired as the Vedas".[6]

God Alone Is

Though Gandhiji has drawn on different religions, he has explained the concept of God, the truth or the ultimate reality mainly in terms of the Hindu Vedantic philosophy. Gandhiji holds the world-view that there is one and only one reality called God which has existence, and God is the only pure 'Isness' in this universe and, therefore, Gandhiji says, "He alone is".[7] Gandhiji was so much enamoured by the Isness aspect of the reality that he chose Truth to be the best name of God. "The word *Satya* (Truth) is derived from *Sat*, which means 'being'. Nothing is or exist in reality except Truth. That is why *Sat* or Truth is perhaps the most important name of God. In fact it is more correct to say that Truth is God, than to say that God is Truth. But as we cannot do without a ruler or a general such names of God as 'King of Kings' or 'The Almighty' are and will remain generally current. On deeper thinking, however, it will be realised that *Sat* or *Satya* is the only correct and fully significant name for God".[8]

Truth or existence being one, cannot be divided in parts. It is a non-fragmentable, indivisible, infinite oneness. The unitary reality has neither a beginning nor an end being the only existence. It is all pervasive and is, therefore, immovable, changeless and absolute. In other words, it is beyond time, space and causation.The *Vedas* and the *Upanishads* have described it as the *Brahman* and the *Gita* has referred to it as the *Purushottama*. In agreement with the Vedantic philosophy, Gandhiji holds the view that God is a universal and all pervasive reality. As he says, "He is in every atom about us, around us and within us".[9] Expressing his immovable faith in the timelessness of God, Gandhiji wrote, "My faith runs so very much faster than my reason that I can challenge the whole world and say, God is, was and ever shall be".[10]

The nature of the ultimate reality is absolute Truth, absolute consciousness, absolute Bliss. In the Vedantic terminology, it is called *Sat, Chit, Anand*. Pure Truth, which is without any trace of untruth, is perfect knowledge as nothing remains to be known, having known it. In perfect knowledge, there is absolute Bliss that is everlasting happiness as nothing remains to be achieved. In 1930, Gandhiji wrote from the Yeravda Central Prison, "And where there is Truth, there also is knowledge which is true. Where there is no Truth, there can be no true knowledge. That is why the word *Chit* or knowledge is associated with the name of God. And where there is true knowledge, there is always Bliss *(Ananda)*. There sorrow has no place. And even as Truth is eternal, so is the Bliss derived from it. Hence we know God as *Sat-Chit-Ananda*, one who combines in Himself Truth, Knowledge and Bliss".[11]

Manifestation of the One as Many

The absolute oneness manifests Itself as many and the universe obeying the laws of Time, Space and Causation is created. According to the Vedantic philosophy, creation of the universe is the will *(Sankalp Shakti)* of the supreme reality *Brahman*. As the *Taittiraya Upanishad* says, "He desired. Would that I were many; Let me procreate myself! He performed austerity. Having performed austerity, he created this whole world, whatever there is here".[12] God is the source of all energy which creates, sustains or dissolves the Universe. "As a spider might come out with his thread, as small sparks come forth of the fire, even so from this soul come forth all vital energies, all worlds, all gods, all beings",[13] maintains the *Brihadaranykopnishad.* The *Gita* also supports the view that God only creates and sustains the world. "I am the generator of all; all evolves from me".[14] Gandhiji has explicitly expressed his faith that God is the supreme power which creates the entire universe, the material world and the world of sentient beings, "I do dimly perceive that whilst everything around me is ever changing, ever dying, there is underlying all that change a living Power that is changeless, that holds all together, that creates, dissolves and recreates. That informing Power or Spirit is God".[15] Accepting God to be the source of all energy, Gandhiji says, "God is the source of light and life".[16] He further elaborates in this connection, "The truth is that God is the force. He is the essence of life. He is pure and undefiled consciousness. He is eternal".[17] God is not only the creator of this universe but He is the greatest regulator and controller, also. "He is the law maker, the law and the Executor",[18] writes Gandhiji. Expressing his views regarding God as the universal force, which controls the laws of nature and regulates the working of the universe, he further says, "There is orderliness in the universe, there is an unalterable Law governing everything and every being that exists or lives. It is not a blind law; for no blind law can govern the conduct of living being. . . . That law then which governs all life is God. Law and the Law giver are one".[19] Gandhiji thus describing God as the Supreme Intelligence and the greatest force, all powerful and all knowing, asserts, "There is no doubt that He rules our action and I literally believe that not a blade of grass grows or moves without His will".[20]

God in Everything

The apparent manifoldness of life is not in any way division of the ultimate oneness. As a matter of fact, it is the same unitary reality which appears as diverse objects under different names and forms. The same pure being is enfolded, involved or implicated in all worldly objects. Every single particle contains the whole. God pervades everything like water pervades snow. God and His creation being the same are both perfect. "The Eternal is complete in itself, the finite is complete in itself, one completeness comes out of another completeness. When one completeness is taken from another completeness, completeness itself remains",[21] says the *Brihadaranyak-upnishad.* Gandhiji was particularly fond of the opening verse of the

Ishavasyopnishad which sums up very beautifully the all pervasive nature of God. "Whatever life exists in this world, is the abode of the Lord".[22] The *Gita* contains many *Shlokas* in support of the fact that God is in everything:

'O Bharat! as the one sun illumines the whole earth, the Lord of the field illumines every being of the creation".[23]

"O Arjun ! whatsoever is the seed of all beings, that am I. There is nothing in this sentient and insentient world which is bereft of me".[24]

"O Gudakesha! I am the *Atman* seated in the hearts of all the beings. I am the beginning, the middle and also the end of the beings".[25]

"That eternal *Brahman* has hands and feet, eyes, heads, mouths and ears everywhere. It pervades the entire universe".[26]

The Indefinable Reality

God is in everything. Yet He defies all description. As Gandhiji says, "He is in us and yet above and beyond us".[27] Expressing the paradox, he further writes, "He is one and yet many ; He is smaller than an atom, and bigger than the Himalayas. He is contained even in a drop of the ocean, and yet not even the seven seas can encompass Him".[28] Finding Him to be inexplicable, Gandhiji says, "There is an indefinable mysterious power that pervades everything. I feel it though I do not see it. It is this unseen power which makes itself felt and defies all proof, because it is so much unlike all that I perceive through my senses".[29] Finding that God is not a subject of the senses, Gandhiji surrenders completely and says, "He is above all attributes, Indescribable, Inconceivable, Immeasurable". [30]

The Big Illusion or Maya

If oneness is the Supreme Truth, why do we experience the world to be in fragments. This is the greatest illusion; in Vedantic terminology, *Maya*, which surrounds man. Reality is one, diversity and manifoldness are only appearances. The world of diversity in which everything appears as a self-subsistent entity is merely an appearance due to a person's ignorance that all essentially is one. According to *Maitri Upanishad*, "there are assuredly two forms of *Brahman*: the formed and the formless. Now that which is the formed is unreal; which is formless is real".[31] Gandhiji in his Autobiography writes, "Often in my progress I have had faint glimpses of the Absolute Truth, God, and daily the conviction is growing upon me that He alone is real and all else is unreal".[32] The Absolute reality can be compared to an unfathomable ocean in which human beings, plants, animals, the suns and stars and all the other phenomenon of the Universe are mere waves or eddies. Shankracharya has explained the doctrine of illusion by giving the simile that a piece of rope lying by the wayside appears in the twilight as a snake to the belated traveller.

The Absolute, Unitary, Changeless, Infinite reality appears to be relative, fragmentary, changing and finite through the coloured veil of time, space and causation. The experiential reality for man is through the mind and senses. Everything that comes through the senses must be partial, fragmentary and illusive as the limited senses can never be a perfect instrument to grasp the unbounded reality. The mind functions through the limitations of time, space and causation and, therefore, the conception and interpretation of the partially perceived sense data further becomes erroneous and misleading for man. The observation is, therefore, not real but unreal as it takes place through a conditioned mind. The *Kathopanishad* says, "Not by speech, not by mind, not by sight can He be comprehended".[33] The human mind can never touch the 'Isness' of life as long as it is a prisoner of time. It is capable of operating only in the past and projecting itself into the future. According to modern thinkers, J. Krishnamurti and Vimla Thakar, it is the conditioning of our minds which does not let us come in direct touch with the reality. "The brain cells are also conditioned in specific ways and they react to stimuli according to the conditioning",[34] says Vimla Thakar. In other words, the world appears to be a big illusion as long as the mind is bound to a relative frame of reference, that is the conditioning.

Gandhiji realises that the senses create a delusive picture of the reality and, therefore, he says, "Sense perceptions can be, often are, false and deceptive, however real they may appear to us".[35] The delusion created by the senses does not let us come in touch with the Divinity. "We must ever fail to perceive Him through the senses because He is beyond them. We can feel Him, if we will but withdraw ourselves from the senses. The divine music is incessently going on within ourselves, but the loud senses drown the delicate music which is unlike and infinitely superior to anything we can perceive or hear with our senses",[36] says Gandhiji. Since the mind and senses are limited, it is necessary to transcend them, drop one's finite individual identity and be merged into the vastness of Infinity, in order to realise the Truth. Gandhiji, therefore, says, "If God is vast and boundless as the ocean, how can a tiny drop like man imagine what He is? He can only experience what the ocean is like, if he falls into and is merged in it".[37]

The illusion or the fragmentary phenomenal world is sustained by the 'I' consciousness. It is the very identification of a being with the 'self' which creates the limited 'I' consciousness and separates one from the unlimited. As soon as the self is dropped and 'I' consciousness is transcended, the individuality is merged into the same one, Absolute Reality. Swami Rama Tirtha says, "On waking up to a realisation of truth . . . you can see that all this world was a mere joke, mere plaything, mere illusion, nothing else".[38] So, ultimately, all the Universe is in reality nothing else but one indivisible, indescribable Reality. The apparent manifoldness and changes of life are just an illusion. They do not affect the 'Isness' aspect of the Absolute in any way. "The real infinity, within the outward apparent finite forms of the monad does not change, it multiplies not, it decreases not, it remains the same",[39] declares Swami Rama Tirtha.

Unity in the Manifested Life

The basic unitary nature of the Absolute finds expression in the apparent multiplicity and diversity of the Universe also. On deeper reflection we find that there is Universal unity, inter-dependence and inter-penetration at various levels in the manifested world. Not only that, there is inner unity at the Absolute level, we find sufficient proof of outer unity also at the gross body level, vital body level and psychic body level in this scientific age. The science of ecology shows that there is inter-dependence and inter-connection, a unity in cyclic order among the mineral, vegetable and animal kingdoms, through the agents of the earth, water and air. We have unity not only with all that exists on the earth, dead or living, animate or inanimate, visible or invisible but also with the Sun, the Moon, the Mars and other planets. The various parts in nature are working continuously to help each other due to the inner thread of continued unity for the common good of the whole. Life is, therefore, not in parts but it is one whole. The whole creation is one vast living organism, a biological unit. Absolute Truth which is ever-existing and all-pervading, when manifested, thus creates a Universe which is vertically and horizontally, one organic homogeneous whole. It is like a big dance of the Lord with His own self expressed as different forms. Diversity is sustained by unity like a lotus flower by its stem. To use Gandhiji's words, "I believe in absolute oneness of God and therefore also of humanity. What though we have many bodies? We have but one soul. The rays of the Sun are many through refraction. But they have the same source".[40]

Love, the Law of Life

Evolution is the law of nature. The entire creation is evolving towards its source, the ultimate oneness, the Absolute Truth. In Gandhiji's words, "I subscribe to the belief or the philosophy that all life in its essence is one, and that the humans are working consciously or unconsciously, towards the realisation of that identity".[41] The world emanates from God and merges back into the same infinite ocean after having completed the cycle of evolution. Gandhiji discovered that it was the law of love which operated throughout as the basic principle of evolution. Absolute Truth of oneness becomes the law of love when manifested, Law and Law-giver are the same according to Gandhiji. Love is implicit in Truth and, therefore, Gandhiji says, "Love may be deduced from Truth, or may be paired with Truth. Truth and love are one and the same thing".[42] Universal force of love unites the seemingly different parts of the universe, designs and organises the various phenomena, maintains order and regularity and carries forward the process of evolution. Gandhiji feels that the force of love is like the cohesive force in matter which holds together the various atoms, "Scientists tell us that without the presence of the cohesive force amongst the atoms that comprise this globe of ours, it would crumble to pieces and we cease to exist; and even as there is cohesive force in blind matter, so must there be in all things animate and the name for that cohesive force among animate beings is love".[43] Though there is the existence of destructive force also, yet the world goes on. Evolution takes place only because the force of love is more than the force of destruction. Gandhiji says, "I believe that the sum total of the energy of mankind is not to bring us down but to lift us up, and that is the result of the definite, if unconscious, working of the law of love. The fact that mankind persists shows that the cohesive force is greater than the disruptive force, centripetal force is greater than the centrifugal".[44] He further contends, "If love was not the law of life, life would not have persisted in the midst of death. Life is a perpetual triumph over the grave".[45] Greater and greater recognition of the law of love is the other name of evolution, "If there is a fundamental distinction between man and beast, it is the former's progressive recognition of the law and its application in practice to his own personal life".[46] Gandhiji was sure that love is the constructive force and that hatred leads to destruction and that ultimately man must take to the path of love. He thus concludes, "I have reasoned out the doctrine of the sword, I have marked out its possibilities and come to the conclusion that man's destiny is to replace the law of the jungle with the law of conscious love".[47]

The holistic approach enkindled in Gandhiji an incessant flame of pure love for the whole of mankind and his whole life was spent in obeying the law of love. Love was the only source of all his activities in all the fields and, therefore, his life was one indivisible whole, there being no fragments or watertight compartments in life. "My life is one indivisible whole and all my activities run into one another and they all have their rise in my insatiable love for mankind",[48] he declared. The holistic world-view led Gandhiji to Universal love which in action became service to humanity. "The only way to find God is to see Him in His creation and be one with it. This can only be done by service of all. I am part and parcel of the whole, and I cannot find Him apart from the rest of humanity".[49]

The same absolute Truth smiles through everyone, big or small, beautiful or ugly, rich or poor, sentient or insentient. The same thread of unity runs through everyone and everything. The unity or wholeness of life is of such a nature that the moment we touch it from any angle, we touch the whole, no single part remaining unaffected. Law of love requires that the apparently different parts must work in close cooperation in a balanced way with the common objective of safeguarding the security, welfare and progress of the whole. The natural regulating force does not stand violation of the law of Love in any way. Treatment of life in fragments, over-emphasis or neglect of any part is bound to create friction, pain and suffering in the world. Whenever there is imbalance or disorder, the force of truth appears in some form or the other in order to prevent injustice, restore order and maintain equanimity. Lord Krishna has declared in the *Gita* in unequivocal terms, "When there is decay of righteousness and exaltation of unrighteousness, I manifest myself in some form or the other to protect the virtuous and to destroy the evil doers".[50] Gandhiji feels that evil and physical calamities have a divine purpose behind them; they come to mankind as chastisement for their sins. God is the greatest life ordering force and so Gandhiji forcefully asserts, "He is patient but He is also terrible. He is the most exacting personage in the world and the world to come. He metes out the same measure to us as we mete out to our neighbours — men and brutes. With him ignorance is no excuse".[51]

To those who turn to Him, God is merciful and compassionate. Gandhiji had experienced that in times of great difficulties God appears to him as Inner Voice or some unforeseen help at the eleventh hour. He says, "On all occasions of trial, He has saved me. . . . When every hope is gone, 'when helpers fail and comforts flee', I find that help arrives somehow, from I know not where. Supplication, worship, prayer are no superstitions, they are acts more real than the acts of eating, drinking, sitting or walking".[52]

Science and Spirituality

The twentieth century developments in Science lend a great deal of support to the Gandhian world-view. The fragmentary, mechanistic view of the matter has been transcended and now Science is leading us towards holistic concept of the Universe which is very much similar to the Gandhian concept of Truth. Physicist Pritjof Capra writes in preface to his work 'The Turning Point', "The new concepts in physics have brought about a profound change in our world-view; from the mechanistic conception of Descrates and Newton to a holistic and ecological view, a view that I have found to be similar to the views of mystics of all ages and traditions".[53]

Universe — A Unified Whole

According to the discoveries of Quantum Physics, the constituents of matter are not discrete, solid, unpenetrable, inert, independently existing parts. At the sub-atomic level everything is interconnected and inter-related. As Capra explains, "Subatomic particles, then, are not 'things' but are inter-connections between 'things', and these 'things', in turn, are inter-connections between other 'things', and so on. In quantum theory you never end up with 'things', you always deal with interconnections. This is how modern physics reveals the basic oneness of the universe. It shows that we cannot decompose the world into independently existing smallest units. As we penetrate into matter, nature does not show us any isolated building blocks, but rather appears as a complicated web of relations between the various parts of a unified Whole".[54]

The particles at the sub-atomic level are not connected by causal laws. The units of matter at that level are very abstract entities which have a dual aspect, sometimes appearing as particles, sometimes as waves, depending upon the consciousness of the observer. Moreover, matter at the sub-atomic level does not exist with certainty at definite places, but rather shows tendencies to exist and so there is indeterminacy in the behaviour of matter. Thus the conception of universe that emerges is that of an interconnected web of relations which is intrinsically dynamic. Capra, therefore, concludes, "Quantum theory has shown that sub-atomic particles are not isolated grains of matter but are probability patterns, interconnections in an inseparable cosmic web that includes the human observer and her consciousness".[55]

David Bohm holds the view that the universe is a gigantic hologram, with each part being in the whole and the whole being in each part. Under the explicable realm of separate things is an implicate realm of undivided wholeness, and this implicate whole is simultaneously available to each explicate part. Drawing a parallel between the world of matter and the world of mystics, he says, "Relativity and, even more important, quantum mechanics have strongly suggested (though not proved) that the world cannot be analysed into separate and independently existing part. Moreover, each part somehow involves all the others; contains them or enfolds them. In this sense, a common language may be said to have been established and a common set of basic concepts, for this is the one point on which all mystics have agreed. This fact suggests that the sphere of ordinary material life and the sphere of mystical experience have a certain shared order and that this will allow a fruitful relationship between them".[56]

The Illusory Perception

At the sub-atomic level, observation includes the observer in an essential way. The consciousness of the observer alters the observation. The objective description of nature is no longer valid. The perception of objects is therefore not absolute but relative. According to Dr. D.S. Kothari, "No longer it is possible, permissible to make sharp distinction of subject and object, between the knower and the things to be known".[57] The implication is that observation will always be illusory as long as the mind is in motion or the observer does not go into abeyance.

According to the relativity theory, space is not three dimensional and time is not a separate entity. Both are intimately connected and form a 'space-time' continuum. Space and time are not absolute and, therefore, all space and time measurements are relative. In other words, all objects of the world bound within the framework of time and space as grasped by the limited senses are relative and therefore unreal, the real being beyond time and space. Gandhiji has, therefore, rightly observed, "He alone is real, all else is unreal".[58]

The Indescribable Reality

The structure of the atoms is so complex that it defies all descriptions. The particles at the sub-atomic level are not connected by causal laws. Space penetrates matter and the atoms instead of being hard and indestructible consist of vast regions of space in which extremely small particles whirl around at fantastic speed ranging from 600 miles per second to 4000 miles per second. Robert Oppenheimer says, "If we ask for instance, whether the position of the electron remains the same, we must say 'no', if we ask whether the electron's position changes with time we must say 'no', if we ask whether the electron is at rest, we must say 'no', if we ask whether the electron is in motion, we must say 'no'".[59] The description is remarkably similar to the statement given by the *Upanishads, "Neti, neti*",[60] (not this, not this) regarding the nature of the ultimate Reality.

Concept of Man and the Purpose of Life

Mahatma Gandhi gives a new concept of man based on the holistic view of life. Man is a part of a whole and has wholeness enfolded within him. He is not just a material being whose existence is limited to the level of mind and body only, he has an unlimited spiritual existence also. At the spiritual level, man has unity with all the other human beings, the animals, the plants, the sun and the stars and everything else that exists. Gandhiji believes, "Man's essence, which is Atman, is all pervading, for he who has realised it, will not see himself as different from others, but will see all in himself".[61]

Gandhiji considers man to be potentially divine. Man has the capability to transcend the mechanistic structure of mind and body and realise the wholeness lying dormant within him. He becomes a prisoner of the 'self', the sensual and psychological structures, but has the potentiality in him to free himself from the shackles of the 'self' and become rooted in the Truth, the pure, sinless state. To quote Gandhiji, "I believe it to be possible for every human being to attain that blessed and indescribable sinless state in which he feels within himself the presence of God to the exclusion of everything else".[62]

Man must reach the highest and, therefore, Gandhiji feels that the purpose of man's life is self-realisation. He states in unambiguous terms, "The purpose of life is undoubtedly to know oneself".[63] Man is not simply a material being and, therefore, endless pursuit of materialism cannot be the ultimate purpose of his life. "He is born day after day not to explore avenues for amassing riches and to explore different means of livelihood; on the contrary, man is born in order that he may utilise every atom of his energy for the purpose of knowing his Maker".[64]

The purpose of Gandhiji's life was self-realisation for which he continuously struggled. In his Autobiography, he writes, "What I want to achieve, what I have been striving and pining to achieve these thirty years — is self-realisation, to see God face to face, to attain *Moksha*. I live and move and have my being in pursuit of this goal".[65] Gandhiji feels deep agony within at the thought that he is still far from God. Expressing his torture, he writes, "It is an unbroken torture for me that I am still so far from Him, Who, as I fully know, governs every breath of my life, and whose off-spring I am".[66] Gandhiji worshipped God as Truth, the all-pervasive 'Isness'. Self-realisation, therefore, meant for him the same as realisation of Truth. He was prepared to sacrifice even his life in the pursuit of Truth. He writes, "I am but an humble seeker after truth and bent upon finding it. I consider no sacrifice too great for the sake of seeing God face to face. The whole of my activity whether it may be called social, political, humanitarian or ethical is directed to that end".[67]

Shedding the Self

Moksha was the purpose of Gandhiji's life because he had a yearning for Absolute Freedom. Like Swamy Vivekananda, freedom was the song of his life. He wanted freedom from all the limitations of an ephemeral and temporal existence. This meant freedom from the limitations of the body and also the limitations of a conditioned mind which express themselves as passions, animal urges and other selfish desires. He wanted to efface his little 'self' so that he may merge himself into the ocean of eternity and hence he often repeated, "I must reduce myself to zero".[68] Gandhiji felt that the 'self' acts as an obstruction in our union with God and, therefore, we must become free of the same. "Our existence as embodied beings is purely momentary; what are hundred years in eternity? But if we shatter the chain of egoism, and melt into the ocean of humanity, we share its dignity",[69] he maintained. Gandhiji's quest was from bondage to freedom, from ignorance to enlightenment, from mortality to immortality.

Growing into the Dimension of Love

Shedding the self is the same as growing into dimension of love. As soon as the self is dropped, limited consciousness expands, and identifies itself with the highest and the lowest simultaneously. The vacuum created by the 'zero' state is filled by the purest energy of absolute love for the whole of mankind. A new human being is born after growing into the dimension of love. The cosmic vision or the holistic perception leads to the cultivation of qualities like compassion, sacrifice, service, cooperation, humanity and fearlessness in man in the place of negativities like greed, hatred, violence, competition, conflict, etc. Explaining the behaviour of a man on the path of selflessness, Gandhiji writes, "When self is shed, the change will be reflected in our outward behaviour. It will show in the littlest of our little acts. The whole outlook on life will be changed. Everything we do will be undertaken not for the little self, but for all".[70] Gandhiji looks at man as a being whose destiny is to gradually move towards selflessness or perish. He explains the historical process of evolution as follows:

> "If we turn our eyes to the time of which history has any record down to our time, we shall find that man has been steadily progressing towards ahimsa. Our remote ancestors were cannibals. Then came a time when they were fed up with cannibalism and they began to live on chase. Next came a stage when man was ashamed of leading the life of a wandering hunter. He, therefore, took to agriculture and depended principally on mother earth for his food. Thus from being a nomad, he settled down to a civilised

stable life, founded villages and towns, and from member of a family he became member of a community and a nation. All these are signs of a progressive *ahimsa* and diminishing hinsa. Had it been otherwise, the human species should have been extinct by now even as many of the lower species have disappeared. . . . Man as animal is violent but as spirit he is non-violent. The moment he awakes to the spirit within, he cannot remain violent. Either he progresses towards *Ahimsa* or rushes to his doom".[71]

E.F. Schumacher writes in his book *A Guide for the Perplexed* that man is a being with unlimited potentialities and therefore he must do 'inner work' to bring out his hidden treasure and become a perfect human being. To explain his point, Schumacher divides everything in the world into four levels of beings: mineral, plant, animal and human, defining them as m, $m + x$, $m + x + y$, $m + x + z$. The factors, m, x, y, z represent matter, life, consciousness and self-awareness. He holds that the four elements are ontological, that is, in their fundamental nature different, incomparable, incommensurable and discontinuous. Therefore, there is a hierarchic order in the world and there is a quantum jump in reaching a 'higher' level of being from a lower level. Schumacher further holds that 'z' which is self-awareness is unlimited and therefore every man can move higher and higher in the progression series by adding to or developing his 'z' faculty. To quote Schumacher, "At the human level, we can clearly perceive that it is open-ended. There is no discernible limit to what man can do; he seems to be *capax universi*, as the ancients used to say and what one person has done henceforth shines like a light in darkness as a capability of man. even if no second person is ever found able to do it again".[72]

Truth and Non-Violence

Gandhiji was basically a man of action and not simply a visionary. There was no gap between his thought and action; he lived and died for the realisation of Truth, which he thought to be the highest state of human life. As he writes, "Devotion to this Truth is the sole justification for our existence. All our activities should be centred in Truth. Truth should be the very breath of our life".[73] How can Truth be realised. The holistic approach of Gandhiji did not allow him to go to the forests and search for Truth sitting in some cave. As he explains, "I have no desire for the perishable kingdom of earth. I am striving for the kingdom of Heaven which is *Moksha.* To attain my end, it is not necessary for me to seek the shelter of a cave. I carry one about me, if I would but know it. A cave dweller who hovers round the world on the wings of thought has no peace".[74] God is a non-fragmentable reality and therefore He is to be sought in everything, everywhere, in every field of activity. The whole creation is like our own extended self; Gandhiji, therefore, sought identification or oneness in a sacred bond of love with all that exists. "I want to realise brotherhood or identity not merely with the beings called human, but I want to realise identity with all life, even with such things as crawl upon earth. I want, if I don't give you a shock, to realise identity with even the crawling things upon earth, because we claim descent from the same God, and that being so, all life in whatever form it appears must be essentially one".[75]

Gandhiji thus arrived at the principle of pure love as a means to realise God, the Absolute Truth. He explicitly states, "To see the universal and all-pervading Spirit of Truth face to face one must be able to love the meanest of creation as oneself. And a man who aspires after that cannot afford to keep out of any field of life".[76] Taking non-violence *(ahimsa)* and love to be one and the same thing, Gandhiji held that non-violence is the means and Truth is the end. Violence, that is violation of Truth, the law of unity of life, is the animal instinct and therefore man must practise non-violence in order to outgrow the brute in him and evolve into the dignity of a holistic man. Gandhiji emphasised non-violence because, "Non-violence is the law of our species as violence is the law of the brute. The spirit lies dormant in the brute and he knows no law but that of physical might. The dignity of man requires obedience to a higher law - to the strength of the spirit".[77] Man must make continuous efforts to evolve progressively by obeying the law of love.

Non-violence is holistic action, that is action springing out of Truth, the wholeness of life. The transcendence of egoistic consciousness into holistic consciousness requires action according to the understanding of Truth instead of action according to the dictates of the 'self'. Life is to be piloted from a wholeness within and not from fragmented conditioned self-image. In Gandhiji's words, "Man's ultimate aim is the realisation of God, and all his activities, social, political, religious have to be guided by the ultimate aim of the vision of God".[78] Gandhiji was, however, aware that as long as the consciousness is imprisoned in this body and mind frame, Truth will appear differently. His approach was, therefore, from truth to truth; one has to be faithful to one's understanding and keep moving with the fresh understanding of truth arrived at. As long as Absolute Truth is not realised, the truth of one's understanding, the relative truth, must be the guiding star of one's actions. As he writes in his biography, "But as long as I have not realised this Absolute Truth, so long must I hold by the relative truth as I have conceived it. That relative truth must, meanwhile, be my beacon, my shield and buckler. Though this path is strait and narrow and sharp as the razor's edge, for me it has been the quickest and easiest".[79] A sincere, steadfast and selfless pursuit of relative truth is inevitably bound to lead to Absolute Truth. The quest for truth in which there is no trace of self-interest is self-correcting. In *From the Yeravda Mandir*, Gandhiji wrote, "In such selfless search for Truth, nobody can lose his bearings for long".[80] The twin conditions that are required for the enquiry are constant watchfulness and selflessness. One has to be constantly on guard lest the untruth, the unreal, the impurities of mind should become the driving force of one's actions. Gandhiji had turned his whole life into a laboratory for this purpose, screening the truth from untruth, experimenting with it and amending it according to the experience gained. Life, for him, was a series of experiments, to discover the Absolute Truth through non-violence in the light of the relative truth. Truth and non-violence go hand in hand helping each other, the mind becoming purer and purer and the actions more and more non-violent in the process. Truth and non-violence are interdependent, inseparable and indistinguishable and so Gandhiji wrote, "Without *ahimsa* it is not possible to seek and find Truth. Ahimsa and Truth are so intertwined that it is practically impossible to disentangle and separate them. They are like the two sides of a coin, or rather of a smooth unstamped metallic disc. Who can say, which is the obverse, and which is the reverse?"[81]

Self-purification or selflessness is an essential condition for the practice of non-violence. Identification with all that exists, or universal love, which is the source of non-violence, cannot develop without purification of the self. Love and selfishness are mutually exclusive, they cannot go together. As Gandhiji says, "Identification with everything that lives is impossible without self-purification; without self-purification the observance of the law of ahimsa must remain an empty dream; God can never be realised by one who is not pure of heart. Self-purification, therefore, must mean purification in all the walks of life".[82] Non-violence, therefore, demands a constant movement towards a state of selflessness. Explaining the path of self-purification, Gandhiji says, "To attain to perfect purity one has to become absolutely passion-free in thought, speech and action; to rise above the opposing currents of love and hatred, attachment and repulsion".[83] The path of self-purification is hard and steep but one has to strive for it ceaselessly if one wants to climb the ladder of evolution.

The first step in the path of non-violence is shedding all hatred in any shape or form and abstaining from hurting any living being in thought, word and deed. Gandhiji warns, "The principle of ahimsa is hurt by every evil thought, by undue haste, by lying, by wishing ill to anybody. It is also violated by our holding on to what the world needs".[84] However, non-violence is not simply a passive state, it is an active engagement in every field of life due to the dynamic and creative force of love. It is a ceaseless occupation with constructive work in every field of individual and collective life whether religious, social, political or economic. It was the force of love for humanity that drew Gandhiji into the field of politics. He says, "If I seem to take part in politics, it is only because politics today encircles us like the coils of a snake from which one cannot get out no matter how one tries. I wish to wrestle with the snake. . . . I am trying to introduce religion into politics".[85]

The spirit of non-violence further connotes that work is worship. Work is not for building up the ego or to get any reward out of it. Work is done in the spirit of selfless service in utter humility and weakness, totally renouncing the fruits of action. Selfless service is rendered like Yagna performed without any desire. Gandhiji following the Nishkam *Karam Yoga* of the *Gita*, emphasises the path of service for God realisation. He says, "The immediate service of all human beings becomes a necessary part of the endeavour simply because the only way to find God is to see Him in His creation and be one with it. This can only be done by service of all".[86] Man's capacity to serve being limited, it is impossible for him to serve the whole of the world's creation. Gandhiji, therefore, suggests that service should be inspired by a '*swadeshi*' spirit; the service of our neighbours being our first and foremost duty. Ignoring the neighbour and seeking to serve people living far away is nothing but 'self' in operation. As the power to serve increases, the field and circle of service may be increased accordingly. Further, Gandhiji has specially emphasised the service of '*Daridranarayana*', that is God appearing in the form of the poor, the underprivileged and the downtrodden. He says, "There is no worship purer or more pleasing to God than selfless service of the poor. The rich in their arrogance and intellectual pride, often forget God and even question His existence. But God dwells among the poor, as they cling to Him as their sole Refuge and Shelter. To serve the poor is, therefore, to serve Him".[87]

The holistic paradigm thus leads Gandhiji to seek the unknown through the known; Gandhiji's quest for Being is in the Becoming. His only purpose of life is no doubt God realisation, but his way to it is through the service of man. The individual aim and social aim thus merge into each other being synchronomous and simultaneous. Gandhiji represents a synthesis of matter and spirit, finite and infinite, means and ends. According to Shri R.R. Diwakar, "In Gandhi, the self, however dominant, dissolved itself on the one hand into the circumference, which was the whole of humanity itself, and, on the other, tapered off into infinity that is God or Truth itself".[88]

Non-violence in its most active form as Truth force does not stand anything contrary to the law of unity of life. There is a determined positive, forceful action in order to resist all untruth, evil, injustice and exploitation in any field of life. In the face of stiff opposition, it becomes *'Satyagraha'*, unattached, selfless adherence to truth, even at the cost of one's life. However, the means adopted to achieve the required ends, never become violent. Gandhiji was concerned with mitigating the suffering of the oppressed, but his holistic approach made him equally concerned with the degradation of the oppressor also. The evil-doer being part of the same unity is within us and is, therefore, to be redeemed with all the love, care and concern at our command. Evil is not to be destroyed by killing but by enlightening the hearts that are plunged into the darkness of hatred, through suffering and self-sacrifice. Gandhiji thus writes, "In the application of *Satyagraha*, I discovered in the earliest stages that pursuit of Truth did not admit of violence being inflicted on one's opponent, but that he must be weaned from error by patience and sympathy. For, what appears to be truth to the one may appear to be error to the other. And patience means self-suffering. So the doctrine came to mean vindication of Truth, not by infliction of suffering on the opponent but one's own self".[89] Non-violence is not cowardice; it is in fact the summit of bravery. "Non-violence in its dynamic condition means conscious suffering", observed Gandhiji, "It does not mean meek submission to the will of the evil-doer, but it means the pitting of one's whole soul against the will of the tyrant".[90] To oppose the tyrant with soul force without indulging in violence of any kind, undergoing supreme suffering is the act of highest bravery. He, therefore, declares, "Non-violence is not a cover for cowardice but it is the supreme virtue of the brave. Exercise of non-violence requires far greater bravery than that of swordsmanship. Cowardice is wholly inconsistent with non-violence".[91]

Gandhiji considers non-violence to be a mighty weapon to fight evil, even an infinitesimal fraction of which is capable of doing wonders. Throwing light on the working of the force of non-violence in rooting out evil, he wrote, "The non-violence of my conception is a more active and more real fighting against wickedness than retaliation whose very nature is to increase wickedness. I contemplate a mental and therefore a moral opposition to immoralities. I seek entirely to blunt the edge of the tyrant's sword, not by putting up against it a sharper-edged weapon, but by disappointing his expectation that I would be offering physical resistance. The resistance of the soul that I should offer instead would elude him. It would at first dazzle him and at last compel recognition from him, which recognition would not humiliate him but would uplift him".[92]

The path of non-violence for realisation of Truth led Gandhiji to arrive at certain principles to guide human behaviour and relationship. These principles or norms of life have a universal application and stand the test of truth in all times and places. A seeker after truth must lead life in accordance with these principles in order to prepare himself for the path of truth and be successful in the mission. Moreover, these principles must serve as the bedrock for social, political and economic structures to create a society based on truth, promoting the evolution of man. The principles suggested by Gandhiji may be counted as truth, ahimsa, non-stealing, non-possession, fearlessness, *brahmacharya*, control of the palate, removal of untouchability, bread labour, tolerance, humility, *swadeshi* and trusteeship. The first six are an important part of almost all the religions in the world; they are known as *Yamas* in the *Patanjali Yog Darshan*, being essential as a preparation for the path of *Yoga*. Gandhiji had proposed the rest of the principles himself in the light of his own experience keeping in view the special social, economic and political conditions in India. Gandhiji had emphasised the importance of unflinching determination and a strong will-power for the realisation of Truth and had therefore suggested the acceptance of these principles as vows *(Vratas)*. According to him, "to do at any cost something that one ought to do constitutes a vow".[93] He thinks that taking vows is not a sign of weakness but it is a bulwark of strength. As long as man is imperfect there will always be a gap between what ought to be done and what is actually done. The taking of vows provides the necessary strength to stick to the path of truth and non-violence in the individual life.

Gandhiji has emphasised effort *(Purushartha)* with full strength and determination in order to reach the set goal, but keeping in view man's limitations, he has given due importance to prayer. God is the ultimate source of all the strength and energy; man being imperfect must always pray to Him for strength and success in his efforts, Gandhiji feels that prayer is intended to sober and humble us and enable us to realise that nothing happens without His will. He says, "Our prayer is a heart search. It is a reminder to ourselves that we are helpless without His support. No effort is complete without prayer, without a definite recognition that the best human endeavour is of no effect if it has not God's blessings behind it".[94] Therefore, he who craves for the awakening of the divine in him must surrender and fall back upon prayer. However, prayer is not simply repetition of God's name or some *'Mantra'* with lips. It is getting into communion with the divine with the whole of one's being, body, mind and soul. As Gandhiji says, "It is better in prayer to have a heart without words than words without a heart. It must be in clear response to the spirit which hungers for it".[95]

NOTES

1. *Harijan*, May 4, 1938, *The Collected Works of Mahatma Gandhi*, New Delhi, Publications Division, Government of India *(CWMG)*, Vol. 67, 1976, p. 74.
2. *Harijan*, March 6, 1937, CWMG, Vol. 64, 1976, p. 398.
3. Romain Rolland, *Mahatma Gandhi*, 3rd impression, New Delhi, Publications Division, 1976, p. 17.
4. *Young India*, Oct. 6, 1921, *CWMG*, Vol. 21, 1966, p. 246.
5. M.K. Gandhi, *Hind Swaraj or Indian Home Rule*, Ahmedabad, Navjivan Publishing House, 1938, p. 50.
6. *Young India*, Oct. 6, 1921, *CWMG*, Vol. 21, 1966, p. 246.
7. Ibid., March 5, 1925, *CWMG*, Vol. 26, 1967.
8. M.K. Gandhi, *From Yeravda Mandir*, Ahmedabad, Navjivan Publishing House, 1932, p. 1.
9. *Harijan*, Nov. 14, 1936, *My God*, comp. R.K. Prabhu, Ahmedabad, Navajivan Publishing House, 1962, p. 12.
10. *Young India*, Jan. 21, 1926, *CWMG*, Vol. 29, 1968, p. 412.
11. M.K. Gandhi, *From Yeravda Mandir*, op. cit., p. 1.
12. *Taittriya Upanishad*, 2.6.
13. *Brihadaranykopnishad*, 2.1.20.

14. *The Gita*, 10.8.
15. *Young India*, Oct.10, 1928, *CWMG*, Vol. 37, 1970, p. 349.
16. Ibid., Mar. 5, 1925, *CWMG*, Vol. 26, 1967, p. 224.
17. *Harijan*, June 22, 1947, *My God*, op. cit., p. 50.
18. *Harijan*, Feb. 24, 1946, *My God*, op. cit., p. 35
19. *Young India*, Oct. 11, 1928, *CWMG*, Vol. 37, 1970, p. 349.
20. *Harijan*, Mar. 23, 1940, *Selections from Gandhi*, N.K. Bose, Ahmedabad, Navajivan Publishing House, 1948, p. 6.
21. *Brihadaranykopnishad*, 5.1.
22. *Ishavasyopnishad*, 1.
23. *The Gita*, 13.33.
24. Ibid., 10.39.
25. Ibid., 10.20.
26. Ibid., 13.13.
27. *Young India*, Mar. 5, 1925, *CWMG*, Vol. 26, 1967, p. 224.
28. Ibid., Jan. 21, 1926, *CWMG*, Vol. 29, 1968, p. 412.
29. Ibid., Oct. 11, 1928, *CWMG*, Vol. 37, 1970, p. 348.
30. *Harijan*, May 14, 1938, *CWMG*, Vol. 67, 1976, p. 64
31. *Maitri Upanishad*, 6.3.
32. M.K. Gandhi, *An Autobiography or the Story of My Experiments with Truth*, Ahmedabad, Navajivan Publishing House, 1940, p. XI.
33. *Kathopanishad*, 66.12.
34. Vimala Thakar, *Towards Total Transformation*, Ahmedabad, New Order Publishing Co., 1970, p. 59.
35. *Young India*, Oct. 11, 1928, *CWMG*, Vol. 37, 1970, p. 349.
36. *Harijan*, June 13, 1936, *CWMG*, Vol. 63, 1976, p. 58.
37. Ibid., Aug. 18, 1946, *My God*, op. cit., p. 28.
38. Quoted in B.L. Atreya, *Practical Vedant*, Lucknow, Rama Tirtha Pratisthan, 1966, p. 17.
39. Ibid, p. 19.
40. *Young India*, Sept. 9, 1924, *Selections from Gandhiji*, N.K. Bose, Ahmedabad, Navajivan Publishing House, 1948, p. 25.
41. *Gandhiji's Correspondence with the Government* (1942-44) *Selection from Gandhi*, op. cit., p. 26.
42. M. K. Gandhi, *From Yeravda Mandir*, op. cit., p. 13.
43. *Young India*, May 5, 1920, *Truth is God*, Comp. R.K. Prabhu, Ahmedabad, Navajivan Publishing House, 1955, p. 15.
44. *Young India*, Nov. 12, 1931, *Truth is God*, op. cit., p. 16.
45. *Harijan*, Sept. 26, 1936, *CWMG*, Vol. 63, 1976, pp. 320-321.
46. Ibid., p. 321.
47. *Harijan*, July 3, 1937, *CWMG*, Vol. 65, 1976, p. 360.
48. Ibid., Mar. 2, 1934, *The Message of Mahatma Gandhi*, ed. U.S. Mohan Rao, New Delhi, Publications Division, Govt. of India, 1968, p. 23.
49. *Harijan*, Aug. 29, 1936, *CWMG*, Vol. 63, 1976, p. 240.
50. *The Gita*, 4.7.
51. *Young India*, Mar. 5, 1925, *CWMG*, Vol. 26, 1967, pp. 224-225.
52. M.K. Gandhi, *An Autobiography*, op. cit., p. 54.
53. Pritjof Capra, *The Turning Point*, London, Flamingo edition, Potana Paperbacks, 1983, p. XVII.

54. Ibid., p. 69-70.
55. Pritjof Capra, *The Turning Point*, op. cit., p. 83.
56. *The Holographic Paradigm and Other Paradoxes*, ed. Kenwilber, London, Shambhala Publications, 1982, p. 190.
57. D.S. Kothari, *Some Thoughts on Science and Religion*, New Delhi, Shri Raj Krishen Jain Charitable Trust, 1977. p. 16.
58. M. K. Gandhi, *An Autobiography*, op. cit., p. XI.
59. Quoted in Pritjof Capra, *The Tao of Physics*, Fontana/Collins, 1976, p. 157.
60. *Brihadaranyakopanishad*, 2.3.6.
61. M.K. Gandhi, *Service Before Self*, ed. Anand T. Hingorani, Bombay, Bhartiya Vidya Bhawan, 1971, p. 31.
62. *Young India*, Nov. 17, 1921, *CWMG*, Vol. 21, 1966, p. 440.
63. M.K. Gandhi, *Service Before Self*, op. cit., p. 62.
64. *The Hindu*, Oct. 18, 1927, *CWMG*, Vol. 35, 1969, p. 152.
65. M.K. Gandhiji, *An Autobiography*, op. cit., p. X.
66. Ibid, p. XII.
67. *Young India*, Sept. 11, 1924, *The Messages of Mahatma Gandhi*, op. cit., p. 23.
68. M. K. Gandhi, *An Autobiography*, op. cit., p. 383.
69. M. K. Gandhi, *From Yeravda Mandir*, op. cit., p. 30.
70. *Harijan*, Oct. 13, 1946, *Service Before Self*, op. cit., p. 76.
71. *Harijan*, Aug. 11, 1940, *CWMG*, Vol. 72, 1978, p. 350.
72. E.F. Schumacher, *A Guide for the Perplexed*, London, ABACUS ed. Sphere Books Ltd., 1978, p. 152.
73. M.K. Gandhi, *From Yeravda Mandir*, op. cit., p. 1.
74. *Young India*, Apr. 3, 1924, *CWMG*, Vol. 23, 1967, p. 349.
75. Ibid., Apr. 4, 1929, *Truth is God*, op. cit., p. 5.
76. M.K. Gandhi, *An Autobiography*, op. cit., p. 383.
77. *Young India*, Aug. 11, 1920, *CWMG*, Vol. 18, 1965, p. 133.
78. *Harijan*, Aug. 29, 1936, *CWMG*, Vol. 63, 1976, p. 240.
79. M.K. Gandhi, *An Autobiography*, op. cit., p. XI.
80. M.K. Gandhi, *From Yeravda Mandir*, op. cit., p. 3
81. Ibid, p. 6.
82. M.K. Gandhi, *An Autobiography*, op. cit., p. 383.
83. M.K. Gandhi, *From Yeravda Mandir*, op. cit., p. 5.
84. Ibid.
85. Quoted in Romain Rolland, *Mahatma Gandhi*, op. cit., p. 76.
86. *Harijan*, Aug. 29, 1936, *CWMG*, Vol. 63, 1976, p. 240.
87. *Young India*, Feb. 14, 1929, *Service Before Self*, op. cit., p. 69.
88. R.R. Diwakar, *Is Not Gandhi The Answer*, Bombay, Bhartiya Vidya Bhawan, 1966, p. 15.
89. *The Message of Mahatma Gandhi*, op. cit., p. 17.
90. *Young India*, Aug. 11, 1920, *CWMG*, Vol. 18, 1965, p. 133.
91. Ibid., Aug. 12, 1926, *CWMG*, Vol. 31, 1969, p. 292.
92. Ibid., Oct. 8, 1925, *CWMG*, Vol. 28, 1968, pp. 305-306.
93. M.K. Gandhi, *From Yeravda Mandir*, op. cit., p. 33.
94. *Harijan*, June 8, 1935, *CWMG*, Vol. 61, 1975, p. 138.
95. *Young India*, Jan. 23, 1930, *Selection from Gandhi*, 1972, op. cit., p. 12.

5

THE ECONOMIC ENDS

TRUTH IS the goal of life and non-violence is the means to realise it. Life being one indivisible whole, the principles of truth and non-violence must be adhered to in all the fields without any exception. Economics must be subservient to the basic goal of the truth of life and be helpful in its achievement through non-violent means. The holistic paradigm and the values of life arising thereof, led Gandhiji to spell out holistic economics comprising of 'ends' and 'means' that stand radically different from those of modern economics. The whole of Gandhian economics, the principles, policy, analysis and economic structures, finds validity and justification on the holistic grounds only. As Mark Lutz has observed, "His system represents a radical departure from the mainstream of economic thought. No doubt, it becomes remarkably coherent and logical as soon as we accept the axiomatic premises of his world-view".[1]

According to the holistic world-view as discussed in Chapter 4, man is a part of the whole, and not an autonomous, self-sufficing, fragmented being. He is not simply an amalgamation of mind and matter, he has a spiritual existence also which transcends all limitations. Modern economics as analysed in Chapter II, takes man not only to be a fragmentary, limited, material being but also takes him to be mechanistic, strictly governed by the laws of matter. Gandhiji breaks this mechanistic concept of man and declares that man is potentially divine. Man has the capacity to grow into the unlimited dimension of spirit by obeying the law of love which, in other words, is functioning in harmony with the law of evolution.

The realm of the spirit is the realm of freedom; freedom from the shackles of the mind, the mechanistic dictates of the limited 'self'. It is a dimension of absolute love spontaneously arising out of the observance of the principle of unity of life. Truth prevails in the province of the spirit, the wholeness and supreme intelligence reigns. The highest human endeavour and achievement lies in growing into the dimension of the spirit by breaking the shell of the limited self. Gandhiji, therefore, held that the purpose of man's life is truth realisation, to know the nature of his true self and grow into the realm of the truth, the wholeness, the spirit. from that of the matter.

The Motivational Force of Human Behaviour

Non-violence is the means to realise the Truth. The supreme Truth of the unity of life requires identification with all that exists, universal love or the observance of the principle of non-violence. Non-violence is action according to the understanding of truth that is the relative truth. Holistic action according to truth cannot take place as long as one is grounded in the fragmented little 'self'. The observance of non-violence requires the piloting of life with a vision of wholeness and not according to the dictates of the conditioned fragmentary 'self'. The whole dynamics of relationships is to be transformed in the light of truth. In other words, shedding the 'self' progressively is the basic condition for the realisation of truth. Gandhiji has observed, "one has to learn to efface self or the ego voluntarily and as a sacrifice in order to find God".[2] To quote him further, "He resides in our hearts, but if we instal self or ego there, we dethrone 'poor' God. I have here used the epithet 'poor' advisedly. For, although He is the king of kings, most High, Almighty, yet He is at the beck and call of any one who has reduced himself to zero and turns to him in uttermost humility of spirit. Let us, then become poor in spirit and find Him within ourselves".[3]

To Gandhiji, the motivational force of human behaviour is the spirit of reducing the self to zero. Economics, the science which deals with human behaviour, therefore, cannot escape the principle of shedding the self. Since there is wholeness in life, the spiritual law does not operate in isolation, it is to find a simultaneous application in all the fields of life. The economic laws must be consistent with moral laws. To quote Gandhiji, "I do not believe that the spiritual law works on a field of its own. On the contrary it expresses itself only through the ordinary activities of life. It thus affects the economic. the social and the political fields".[4] Gandhian holistic economics, therefore, takes 'self-annihilation' or 'reducing the self to zero' to be the basic driving force of human behaviour. Here Gandhian economics stands in sharp contrast to modern economics which upholds the pursuit of 'self-interest' as being the prime psychological drive in man.

Ethical Values and Economics

'Self-interest', according to modern economics, is deemed not only rational but also desirable. Pursuit of self-interest for the sake of pleasure leads to certain economic values like acquisition, competition, protection, assertion and sensual indulgence, which though implicit, underlie the entire economic thought. On the other hand, according to the Gandhian approach, the pursuit of truth gives rise to certain ethical values like truth, non-violence, fearlessness, non-stealing, non-possession control of the palate, Brahmacharya, bread labour, Swadeshi and trusteeship. Gandhiji suggested the adoption of these values emanating from truth, as principle of life to guide human conduct and relationships. These ethical values, bearing upon economics, lead to profound changes in certain basic economic concepts, economic 'ends' and 'means' which form the warp and weft of economic thought. It is impossible to think of Gandhian economics without ethics which permeates his economic ideas all along the line. Considering life to be one whole, Gandhiji draws no distinction between economics and ethics. In 1921, he wrote, "I must confess that I do not draw a sharp or any distinction between economics and ethics. Economics that hurts the moral well-being of an individual or nation is immoral and, therefore, sinful".[5] Economics that makes bodily welfare its sole objective, ignoring moral and spiritual welfare, is fragmentary and, therefore, sinful and disastrous. In 1937, he asserted, "True economics never militates against the highest ethical standard, just as all true ethics to be worth its name must at the same time be also good economics. An economics that inculcates Mammon worship and enables the strong to amass wealth at the expense of the weak is a false and dismal science. It spells death".[6] Economics that violates morality was in no way acceptable to Gandhiji and so he declared, "That economics is untrue which ignores or disregards moral values".[7]

'What Ought to be?' and 'What is?'

Modern economics is a positive science concerned with 'What is' rather than 'What ought to be'. Robbins takes economics to be a pure science of 'What is', not at all concerned with moral or ethical questions. Since man is a mechanistic being, his behaviour is given and unalterable and, therefore, economics must study man as he 'is'. The pleasure principle and the principle of self-interest will always govern the behaviour of man and, therefore, economics which studies human behaviour must remain to be a positive science. Gandhiji takes a dynamic concept of man, taking him to be a being clothed in the limitations of mind and body but always seeking and rising towards the permanent element, the spirit, the truth, wholeness, which lies dormant in him. *'Swaraj'*, that is the rule of the (higher) self, is the goal of human life. In *'Hind Swaraj'*, Gandhiji says that 'Swaraj' is learning to rule ourselves.[8] Man has to become free of the slavery of the mind and learn to rule his actions by pure intellect, that is, conduct his behaviour according to the principles of truth and non-violence. Self-restraint, morally sanctified conduct, non-exploitation and honest performance of duty in a spirit of selfless service are the important characteristics of the Gandhian economic man. Economic behaviour cannot be contrary to ethical behaviour according to the requirement of the holistic world-view. Gandhian holistic economics is, therefore, a normative science operating within the framework of moral principles, concerned with what 'ought to be', as it studies the behaviour of a man learning to rule himself through self-control for the sake of *'Swaraj'*.

Material Expansion within Optimal Limits

The holistic paradigm and the explicit inclusion of ethical values in economics leads to a profound change in the basic goal of economics. According to modern economics, more and more goods and services are required for the 'betterment', 'happiness' or 'well being' of man, since man is a material being seeking pleasure. Welfare being equated with material advancement, the purpose of economics is unbounded augmentation of wealth or increase in the flow of goods and service now as well as in future. Gandhiji, taking 'spirit' to be the permanent element in man defines the 'well being' of man in terms of spiritual or moral elevation. True happiness lies in achieving moral welfare and not material welfare for its own sake. However, material welfare cannot be ignored, as body and mind are the instruments of service which helps in achieving moral elevation. Material requisites are essential in so far as they are helpful in maintaining a healthy body and bright mind so that all the latent faculties of man may be actualised. The goal of economics is, therefore, not pursuit of unbounded materialism as body is not meant for indulgence and pleasure seeking, but 'provision of optimal amount of goods' in order to keep mechanistic structure in a fit condition of well-being so that through service, the highest potentiality of man to become a complete expression of wholeness may be realised. The scope of economics lies in helping man to maximise his moral well-being with the help of necessary material requisites. In the words of A.M. Huq, "Maximisation of moral and, to the extent necessary, material welfare may be stated as the principle welfare criteria in Gandhian economics".[9]

Material advancement is acceptable to Gandhiji, only in so far as it promotes spiritual elevation. Economic interests must always be subservient and remain supportive and secondary to spiritual interest. The purpose of economics is not pursuit of unbounded material abundance for its own sake and at all costs. The holistic economics thus puts limits of optimality on material expansion. "There was true wisdom in the sages of old, having so regulated society as to limit the material conditions of people",[10] supported Gandhiji. Economics, thus must never be allowed to cut across the path of morality. As summed up by Romesh Diwan and Mark Lutz, "The integrated and holistic perspective in economics boils down to this simple injunction: never advocate actions or policies that lead to ("economic") material advancement at the cost of ("non-economic") social, moral or spiritual impoverishment. instead, the economist as the holistic economist 'should ascertain that his organisational principles and policies enable, possibly even encourage, a higher overall quality of life for all'.[11] In a lecture delivered on December 22, 1916, at a meeting of the Muir College Economics Society in Allahabad, Gandhiji had raised the question, "Does economic progress clash with real progress"? He had explained, "By economic progress, we mean material advancement without limit, and by real progress we mean moral progress, which again, is the same thing as progress of the permanent element in us".[12] Answering the question he had said, "I hold that economic progress in the sense I have put it is antagonistic to real progress. Hence the ancient ideal has been the limitation of activities promoting wealth . . . that you cannot serve God and Mammon is an economic truth of the highest value".[13]

Gandhiji has vehemently criticised modern civilisation which makes 'bodily welfare' the object of life and fails miserably even in doing so. The huger or wealth and the greedy pursuit of worldly pleasures results in "life corroding competition".[14] It leads to the creation of an economic order in which inequality, exploitation, oppression and poverty prevails and human dignity is mutilated and destroyed. Regarding the degradation of life, in this connection, he writes, "Formerly, men worked in the open air only as much as they liked. Now, thousands of workmen meet together and for the sake of maintenance work in factories or mines. Their condition is worse than that of beasts. They are obliged to work, at the risk of their lives, at most dangerous occupation, for the sake of millionaires. Formerly, men were made slaves under physical compulsion. Now they are enslaved by temptation of money and of the luxuries that money can buy". He further asserts, "This civilisation is irreligious and it has taken such a hold on the people in Europe that those who are in it appear to be half mad. They lack real physical strength or courage. They keep up their energy by intoxication. They can hardly be happy in solitude". This civilisation takes note neither of morality nor of religion, being based on a fragmentary world-view. Gandhiji, therefore, forcefully condemns "This civilisation is such that one has only to be patient and it will be self-destroyed. According to the teaching of Mohammed this would be considered a Satanic Civilisation. Hinduism calls it the Black age. . . . It must be shunned".[17]

True civilisation is that mode of conduct which points to man the path of duty. Performance of duty is observance of morality which means to attain mastery over our mind and passions. Gandhi, therefore, is in favour of ancient Indian civilisation which sets a limit to our indulgence, dissuades us from the economic philosophy of more and more and thus contributes to our moral welfare which is the source of true happiness. In 1938, Gandhiji wrote in 'Hind Swaraj', "The tendency of the Indian civilisation is to elevate the moral being, that of the Western Civilisation is to propagate immorality. The latter is godless, the former is based on a belief in God. So understanding and so believing, it behoves every lover of India to cling to the old Indian civilisation even as a child clings to the mother's breast".[18]

Fulfilment of Needs: Deliberate Restriction of Wants

Truth requires that wants should be scientifically explored, pruned and regulated in the light of wholeness. They cannot be taken for granted blindly, as they arise in the mind due to the operation of self-interest. An alert, bright and sensitive mind which is rooted in wisdom puts a deliberate restriction on wants. A mechanistic mind which is enslaved to the dictates of the self-interest gives rise to the multiplicity of wants. The quest for truth makes man 'need' oriented whereas the pursuit of self-interest makes him 'want' oriented. The purpose of consumption is not pursuit of pleasure arising out of the satisfaction of unlimited wants but the fulfilment of 'needs' which are essential for the maintenance of body and development of mind so that man may become an effective instrument of service to mankind. Gandhiji, therefore, denounced the unlimited character of wants and advocated fulfilment of needs. The conventional economics as discussed in Chapter 2, not only accepts but also deems desirable the multiplicity of wants. The holistic perspective leads to a voluntary reduction of wants to the levels of needs. The basic principles underlying the theory of voluntary and deliberate restriction of wants are the principles of ahimsa, non-stealing and non-possession.

The Principle of Ahimsa

"The principal of *ahimsa*", observed Gandhiji, "is violated by our holding on to what the world needs".[19] A seeker after truth has to tread the path of love and non-violence; there has to be an identification with all that exists; a tender concern for the fellow beings. Love and a callous indifference to the miseries of others do not go together. Economics of love, therefore, requires that so long as there is hunger and poverty in the world, minimum needs only must be fulfilled. "If we are to be non-violent", says Gandhiji, "we must then not wish for anything on this earth which the meanest or the lowest of human beings cannot have".[20] The essence of religion is self-sacrifice; an individual growing into the dimension of wholeness will never seek multiplication of wants as long as the dire needs of the poor go unsatisfied. "The religion of ahimsa consists in allowing others the maximum of convenience at maximum of inconvenience to us, even at the risk of life".[21] The consumer should not choose to think of getting what he can; rather he should decline to receive what others cannot have.

The Principle of Non-Stealing

The principle of non-stealing which forms the basis of the theory of voluntary restriction of wants, is directly derived from the holistic paradigm. God is the creator of everything in this world and, therefore, everything belongs to God. Since all the human beings are the manifestation of the same power of Truth, all the material goods in the world are to be shared equally by all. No individual has the right to consume or possess more than his proportionate share. Thus, one who takes more than one's due share is guilty of committing 'theft'. A seeker after truth cannot steal and simultaneously claim to follow truth or cherish love. Gandhiji has further observed that it is theft to take anything of which we have no real need. The assumption underlying the theory of needs is that God creates enough to satisfy our needs and nothing more; hence, the observance of the principle of non-stealing would require that only real needs are to be fulfilled. Gandhiji has pointedly said, "The profound truth upon which the observance is based is that God never creates more than what is strictly needed for the moment. Therefore, whoever appropriates more than the minimum that is necessary for him is guilty of theft".[22] The breach of the principle of non-stealing is responsible for the poverty and the inequalities of income existing in the world. In 1916, Gandhiji wrote, "I suggest that we are thieves in a way. If I take anything that I do not need for my own immediate use and keep it, I thieve it from some body else. I venture to suggest that it is the fundamental law of Nature, without exception, that Nature produces enough for our wants from day-to-day, and if only everybody took enough for himself and nothing more, there would be no pauperism in this world. There would be no man dying of starvation in this world. But so long as we have got this inequality so long we are thieving".[23] Voluntary restriction of wants and not the multiplication of wants should be the goal of the individual and collective economic life. A perpetual vigilance is required to discriminate needs from wants and a continuous effort is necessary to gradually curtail the superfluous wants. As observed by Gandhiji, "We are not always aware of our real needs, and most of us improperly multiply our wants and thus unconsciously make thieves of ourselves. If we devote some thought to the subject, we shall find that we can get rid of quite a number of wants".[24]

Needless to say that deliberate and voluntary restriction of wants is significantly different from forced poverty, or limitation of wants through the budget line. Voluntary restriction of wants is not a negative activity; it is a positive expression of love for fellow-beings arising out of the holistic vision. Civilisation is growing into the dimension of love and truth. Gandhiji, therefore, denounces modern civilisation based on the materialistic pursuit of self-interest leading to the multiplicity of wants and asserts, "Civilisation, in the real sense of the term consists not in the multiplication, but in the deliberate and voluntary reduction of wants".[25]

Non-Possession or Voluntary Simplicity

The principle of non-possession bears close similarity to the principle of non-stealing. One should not possess more than one's requirement. Truth is ever-existing having no yesterdays and tomorrows. God creates from moment to moment for the needs of his creation. Those who have faith in the existence of Truth will be happy to live in the present without projecting the future; there will be no extra provision for tomorrow. As Gandhiji has declared, "A seeker after Truth, a follower of the law of Love cannot hold anything against tomorrow. God never stores for the morrow; He never creates more than what is strictly needed for the moment. If, therefore, we repose faith in His providence, we should rest assured, that he will give us everyday our daily bread, meaning everything that we require".[26]

In adherence to the law of Love, possession should never go beyond what the others are able to possess. Gandhiji, therefore, says, "Possession seems to me to be a crime. I can only possess certain things which I know that others, who also want to possess similar things, are able to do so".[27] A more positive expression of universal love would mean giving up all your possession for the sake of others. Gandhiji declares, "Love and exclusive possession can never go together. Theoretically when there is perfect love, there must be perfect non possession".[28] In consonance with the principle of non-stealing, the principle of non-possession implies that anything which is not required at a particular time and situation is not to be stored up. "This principle (non-possession) is really a part of non-stealing. Just as one must not receive so must one not possess anything which one does not really need. It would be a breach of this principle to possess unnecessary food-stuffs, clothing or furniture. For instance, one must not keep a chair if one can do without it. In observing this principle, one is led to a progressive simplification of life".[29]

Simplicity or the principle of non-possession does not at all mean that human labour, talents and capabilities are to be underutilised or wasted in any way. They are to be exercised to the maximum extent, in the right direction. As far as wealth is concerned, after keeping minimum for the needs, the rest is to be used for societal welfare. Each will work according to his natural talents and capabilities to the maximum but will take minimum according to his legitimate needs. Similarly, if there is extra wealth in one's possession one will act as a trustee of the same and use it in the best interest of a society. Dispossession is a gradual process and, therefore, one is to be imbued with a spirit of trusteeship regarding one's possessions till the ideal is reached. Explaining the theory of trusteeship in the case of wealth, Gandhiji writes, "Suppose I have come by a fair amount of wealth either by way of legacy, or by means of trade and industry, I must know that all that wealth does not belong to him. What belongs to me is the right to honourable livelihood, no better than that enjoyed by others".[30]

The philosophical roots of the principles of non-stealing and non-possession are to be found in the *Ishavasya mantra*, the first verse of the *Ishopanishad*, Gandhiji was deeply impressed by the *mantra* which he described as the golden key for the solution of all the difficulties and doubts that may assail one's heart. He felt that the whole of the philosophy of religion found in any part of the world is contained in this mantra, and that it excludes everything contrary to it. Gandhiji has spoken at length on this mantra in different contexts. Explaining the meaning of the *mantra* in a speech delivered at *Haripad* in Travancore, he said,

> "All that there is in this universe, great or small, including the tiniest atom is pervaded by God, known as creator of Lord. Isha means the Ruler and he who is the creator naturally by very right become the Ruler too. . . . Thus he (the seer) says, 'Renounce everything, i.e., everything that is on this universe, and not only on this tiny globe of ours, renounce it. He asks us to renounce as we are such insignificant atoms that if we had any idea of possession it would seem ludicrous. And then says the Rishi, reward of the renunciation is *Bhunjitha,* i.e., enjoyment of all you need. But there is a meaning in the word translated 'enjoy', which may as well be translated as 'use', 'eat', etc. it means that you may not take more than is necessary for your growth. Hence this enjoyment or use is limited by two conditions. One is the act of renunciation. . . . And when a man has performed that act of renunciation and dedication, he derives from that act the right of eating, drinking, clothing and housing himself to the extent necessary for his daily life. Therefore, take it as you like, either in the sense that the enjoyment or use is the reward of renunciation, or that the renunciation is essential for our existence, for our soul. And as if that condition given in the mantra was incomplete, the Rishi hastened to complete it by adding. 'Do not covet what belongs to another'."[31]

The observance of the principle of non-violence is, ultimately, selfless service to humanity. Possession which is a means to self-indulgence is contrary to selfless service. Dispossession is, therefore, an essential condition for service leading to self-realisation. It is not easy to understand the difficulties of the poor and serve them without becoming one like them. From the standpoint of pure Truth, body too is a possession, which is to be ultimately dispossessed. Gandhiji thus concludes, "We thus arrive at the ideal of total renunciation and learn to use the body for the purpose of service so long as it exists so much so that service and not bread becomes with us the stuff of life. We eat and drink, sleep and wake for service alone. Such an attitude of mind brings us real happiness and the beatific vision in the fulness of time".[32]

Perfection in love or non-possession or total renunciation will remain an unattainable ideal as long as we are alive like Euclids' definition of a point. But the ideal should always guide human actions and we must ceaselessly strive towards perfection. Gandhiji, therefore, emphasising the fulfilment of minimum needs only, wrote, "Whilst you have the body, you will have to have something to clothe the body with also. But then you will take for the body not all that you can get but the least possible, the least with which you can do, you will take for your house not many mansions but the least cover that you can do with. And similarly with reference to your food and so on".[33]

Maximisation of Happiness, Not Utility

The goal of Gandhian holistic economics is maximisation of happiness and not 'utility' as defined strictly in the economic sense of the term. Utility is dependent upon the consumption of more and more goods only, whereas happiness springs from many other sources besides fulfilment of needs according to Gandhian approach. Work, in modern economics, is all disutility, whereas in Gandhian economics, work is a source of happiness being self-defined and creative. There is more time and opportunity for self-fulfilment and creativity. The individual utility functions are inter-dependent; the happiness of others adds to the happiness of the individual. Service to others is another important source of happiness. Gandhian economic system thus leads to happiness at physical, intellectual and spiritual levels. The production goal of Gandhian economic system is the maximisation of socially necessary goods and services only, yet the happiness obtained is much higher than that under modern economic system, which has before itself the goal of maximising the physical volume of all kinds of goods and services, now as well as in future.

Mahatma Gandhi rejected modern economics on moral as well as economic grounds. Modern 'Acquisitive Society' has not tended to happiness in spite of all its emphasis on multiplicity of wants and accumulation of wealth. The psychological wants for sensual pleasure and psychological wants for egoistic gratification create a pressure on the mind and force man to desire unlimited goods of different variety. The consumption of material goods gives man temporary relief termed as satisfaction or utility. In the process more pressure is built on the mind and senses due to the repetitive tendency of pleasure. Therefore, as soon as the temporary relief is over, hankering for more and more reappears under the push and pull of matter and man, therefore, remains for ever unsatisfied. In *'Hind Swaraj'*, Gandhiji says, "Mind is a restless bird; the more it gets, the more it wants and still remains unsatisfied. The more we indulge in our passions the more unbridled they become".[34] The tendency to accumulate and multiply wants is aggravated by comparison, demonstration, propaganda and advertisements in modern acquisitive societies. However, in the relentless pursuit of matter, man gets only relief, a feeling of filling up an emptiness and no real positive happiness.

Multiplicity of wants beyond a certain limit creates negative feelings like anxiety, fear, envy and frustration. Besides these inner contradictions, outer contradictions are also created. Man is placed against man, society and nature. As discussed in Chapter 3, the economic crisis today encircles the social, political, psychological and ecological life of man. The world faces the problems of poverty, inequalities of income, unemployment, exploitation, alienation and ultimately war. It is becoming increasingly clear that the multiplicity of wants beyond a fair limit does not tend to happiness in the same proportion rather it retards happiness. In a discussion with Maurice Frydman, Gandhiji had said:

> "A certain degree of physical harmony and comfort is necessary but above a certain level, it becomes a hindrance instead of help. Therefore, the ideal of creating an unlimited number of wants and satisfying them seems to be a delusion and a snare. The satisfaction of one's physical needs, even the intellectual needs of one's narrow self, must meet at a point, a dead stop, before it degenerates into physical and intellectual voluptuousness."[35]

Modern economic system faces the problem of scarcity of resources in relation to the multiplicity of wants. The problem of the relative scarcity of world resources confronts us today with all its severity and seriousness. Relentless exploitation of nature as a result of the fragmentary approach has led to the problems of depletion of resources, ecology and pollution. The holistic paradigm takes nature to be a part of the holistic plan and therefore holds nature in reverence. Nature is not to be exploited, plundered and polluted blindly; man must take from it, whatever is required for the fulfilment of needs only. Gandhiji is convinced that this world has enough for everybody's needs but not enough even for one man's greed. A balanced and cooperative relationship with nature makes Gandhian economic system free of the problems of scarcity of resources, ecology and pollution.

Rationality and Minimising Behaviour

The fragmented man in modern economics is guided by maximising behaviour, rationality requires that utility or profit must be maximised for the limited individual self. The holistic man, living in a world of inter-relationship, identifies himself with all the other living beings and, therefore, treats them as his extended self. He shares the happiness, pain and suffering of the fellow-beings. The utility functions in a holistic economy are, therefore, interdependent. The concept of rational economic behaviour, here, undergoes a profound change. Rationality does not lie in maximising behaviour for the limited individual self. The awareness of the extended self leads to a maximising behaviour for the extended self but minimising behaviour for the limited individual self. The holistic man is for ever making an effort to merge his limited self into the extended self. The care and concern for the fellow-beings may not lead the consumer to always buy in the cheapest market to maximise personal utility. Under the Gandhian economic system, a man buys in the local surroundings only, guided by the spirit of Swadeshi. While replying to the question, "Is the economic law that man must buy in the best and the cheapest market wrong"? Gandhiji had categorically replied, "It is one of the most inhuman among the maxims laid down by modern economists. Nor do we always regulate human relations by any such sordid considerations".[36] The holistic man must buy in the local surroundings in order to help the local producers. According to the principle of *Swadeshi*, recognising the physical limitations of man, Gandhiji feels that our first duty is towards our immediate neighbours. To serve one's neighbour is to serve the world. If everybody followed the principle of *Swadeshi* and served his neighbours to the maximum capacity, no one in the world needing help would be left unattended. The principle of *Swadeshi* is to become our guiding star in various fields of activities. In the domain of economics, Gandhiji explains, "I should use only things that are produced by my immediate neighbours and serve those industries by making them efficient and complete where they might be found wanting".[37]

Similarly, inspired by the spirit of Trusteeship, those who own extra wealth, talent and capabilities will invest not to maximise their personal profits but to maximise societal benefits, considering themselves as mere trustees.

Sarvodaya: Welfare of All

The well-being of man lies in his moral elevation and to that extent necessary material welfare. The purpose of holistic economics is provisioning of goods and services to fulfil the physical and intellectual needs of man in an atmosphere of freedom *(Swaraj)* so that the best in man, his creativity, his highest potentiality may find expression. The holistic paradigm implies that part is in the whole and whole is in the part. Therefore, as far as welfare is concerned, whether individual or societal, no single part however small, petty or lowly from the worldly point of view, can be ignored. One of the basic goals of Gandhian holistic economics is, therefore, *Sarvodaya*, the welfare of all, the poor and the downtrodden as well as the rich, the capitalist and the landlord. The fundamental principle of the unity of life suggests that welfare can never be broken in parts; it is an all inclusive concept. So, the welfare of the whole is to be promoted, partial welfare, being against the law of nature is self-defeating. In Gandhiji's words, the doctrine of *Sarvodaya*, may be summed up as follows:

> "If we would see our dream of *Sarvodaya*, i.e., true democracy, realised, we would regard the humblest and lowest Indian as being equally the ruler of India with the tallest in the land. This presupposes that all are pure or will become pure if they are not. No one would then harbour any distinction between community and community, caste and outcaste. Everybody would regard all as equal with oneself and hold them together in the silken net of love."[38]

It was Ruskin's *Unto This Last* that brought about an instantaneous and practical transformation in Gandhiji's life, enabling him to evolve his concept of *Sarvodaya*. He translated the book into Gujarati, entitling it *Sarvodaya* (the welfare of all). Ruskin had felt that the true wealth of a nation is represented by the quality of life of its people. To quote him, "In fact, it may be discovered that the true veins of wealth are purple — and not in Rock, but in Flesh — perhaps even that the final outcome and consummation of all wealth is in the producing as many as possible full-breathed, bright-eyed and happy hearted human creatures".[39] Ruskin, vehemently attacked an economic system based on competition, profiteering and accumulation leading to the exploitation and oppression of man. He passionately spoke against the inhuman economic principles leading to the erosion of human 'life' and values and demanded restructuring of economic and social life in which even the last man would be recognised and given his fair due.

Gandhiji had summed up the teachings of *Unto This Last* in his Autobiography as follows:

(1) That the good of the individual is contained in the good of all.
(2) That a lawyer's work has the same value as the barber's inasmuch as all have the same right of earning their livelihood from their work.
(3) That a life of labour, i.e., the life of the tiller of the soil and the handicraftsman, is the life worth living.[40]

In economic terms, *Sarvodaya* would mean that everyone without any exception must be assured a minimum standard of living, that is, a balanced diet, a decent house to live in, sufficient cloth and adequate educational and medical facilities. Provisioning of the minimum necessities of life for the masses is economic *Swaraj* which negatively speaking implies absence of all exploitation, deprivation and oppression. Gandhiji's attention was, however, especially captured by the last one on the socio-economic ladder, that is, the hungry, the poor, the exploited and the down-trodden. "The *Swaraj* of my dream is the poor man's *swaraj*",[41] said Gandhiji. *Swaraj* is not *'Poorna Swaraj'* until basic amenities are guaranteed to the poorest of the poor. Gandhiji observed that for the poor the economic is the spiritual, God to the poor appears only as bread. To quote him, "I dare not take before them the message of God. I may as well place before the dog over there the message of God as before those hungry millions who have no lustre in their eyes and whose only God is their bread. I can take before them a message of God only by taking the message of sacred work before them. It is good enough to talk of God whilst we are sitting here after a nice breakfast and looking forward to a nicer luncheon, but how am I to talk of God to millions who have to go without two meals a day? To them God can only appear as bread and butter".[42] Gandhian welfare criterion, therefore, implies that the needs of the hungry, the poor, the starving, the last one must get the topmost priority. In 1928, Gandhiji wrote in *Young India*, "According to me the economic constitution of India and for that matter that of the world, should be such that no one under it should suffer from want of food and clothing".[43]

Maximisation of moral welfare, and material welfare necessary for the same, is the principle welfare criterion in Gandhian holistic economics. However, the welfare criterion is to be applied to all without any exception and not just to the majority in a society. According to modern economics, the maximum happiness of the maximum number is the principle goal to be achieved. Accepting the 'Compensation principle', the welfare of a society is measured by the total amount of goods and services enjoyed by its people. An economy is said to be growing in welfare if its annual social product is increasing, even though it has millions of people who are hungry, illiterate and dying of disease and starvation. The holistic paradigm considers each individual to be an expression of Wholeness, the Truth, the God. When one individual suffers, the whole society suffers. The suffering of a hungry, starving individual is indefinite and, therefore, it can never be compensated by making the others better off in any way. There is unlimited potentiality in every human being, so even if one life whithers away without blossoming, there is an unlimited loss to the society. Denouncing the Benthamite principle of greatest good of the greatest number, Gandhiji said, "I do not believe in the doctrine of the greatest good of the greatest number. It means, in its nakedness, that in order to achieve the supposed good of 51 per cent, the interest of 49 per cent may be, or rather should be, sacrificed. The only real, dignified human doctrine is the greatest good of all, and this can only be achieved by uttermost self-sacrifice".[44] The good of the individual, therefore, can be in no way neglected.

As suggested by Romesh Dewan and Sushila Gidwani, according to Gandhian economics, societal utility function is maximised through maximisation of the number of economically satisfied individuals.[45] In fact the holistic approach advocates a harmonious development of the individual and the society. The individual must sacrifice his interest for the sake of society and the society must look after the interests of the individual.

Socialism and Equality

Socialism is embedded in the holistic paradigm. The socialistic ideal of equality is an essential part of Gandhian Sarvodaya. God is the creator of all and, therefore, each human being has an equal status in the holistic plan. Whatever the differences, they have been created by man and, therefore, they must be unmade by man. Explaining the concept of socialism, Gandhiji said, "Socialism is a beautiful word, and so far as I am aware, in socialism all the members of society are equal — none low, none high. In the individual body the head is not high because it is the top of the body, nor the soles of the feet low because they touch the earth. Even as members of body are equal, so are the members of society. This is socialism. In it the prince and the peasant, the wealthy and the poor, the employer and the employee are all on the same level".[46] The aim of socialism is established of a classless, sectionless society in which all the individuals have equal right to welfare and opportunity for self-development. Gandhiji asserted, "I want to bring about an equalisation of status. The working classes have all these centuries been isolated and relegated to a lower status. They have been Shudras and the word has been interpreted to mean an inferior status. I want to allow no differentiation between the son of a weaver, of an agriculturist and of a school master".[47] Gandhiji believed that *Swaraj* cannot be sustained without economic equality. He asserts, "Economic equality is the master key to non-violent independence. Working for economic equality means abolishing the eternal conflict between capital and labour. It means the levelling down of the few rich in whose hands is concentrated the bulk of the nation's wealth, on the one hand, and the levelling up of the semi-starved naked millions, on the other".[48] Gandhian Socialism in its fulness implies equality, justice, love, dignity of human personality and complete absence of exploitation and oppression of any member of society.

Socialism emerged in the West as a reaction to individualism in the eighteenth century. Poverty, inequalities of income, exploitation, misery and human degradation during that period roused the human and fellow feelings of thinkers like St. Simon, Fourier, Proudhon,

Robert Owen, Louis Blanc and Lassalle. These socialist thinkers conceived of and sincerely worked for anew social order based on the principles of equality and justice. However, the attempts of these early socialists proved abortive as they did not have a proper foundation and lacked the necessary goal and conviction to bring about a change in human nature. Later on Marx, again pained by the misery and suffering of the masses, came out with his scientific socialism known as Communism cherishing the ideals of equality and justice. As a disciple of Hegel, Marx believed that change is a dialectical process. The struggle between thesis and antithesis gives rise to synthesis which in turn further creates thesis and antithesis and the process of change thus goes on and on. Marx being a materialist believed that the economic factors determine and shape the evolutionary process. He looked at progress as an outcome of the struggle between the economic classes, the bourgeoisie and the proletariat in his times. He believed that all efforts should be made to intensify the struggle, so that the process of change may be hastened and, therefore, he appealed to the workers of the world to unite and overthrow the capitalists and capture the means of production even through a bloody revolution.

The goals of Gandhian socialism and Marxian communism are very much similar. In fact, Gandhiji sometimes called himself a socialist and a communist though with a difference. However, there are certain essential differences between communism and Gandhian socialism. The roots of Gandhian socialism lie in the fundamental principle of unity of life, whereas communism looks at it only as a historical necessity. Gandhiji had great faith in the transformation of human nature, however, he did not rule out the possibility of a revolution if man fails to transform himself. The holistic paradigm does not lend support to the pursuit of materialism, whereas socialism and communism seek unlimited materialism for a particular group or a nation. The communists adopt violent and bloody means in order to hasten the process of change leading to their cherished goals. For Gandhiji, means are the ends in themselves. Gandhian Socialism, based on the holistic paradigm, takes even the enemy within its fold and favours only those means which are pure and non-violent. Gandhiji said, "This socialism is as pure as crystal. It, therefore, requires crystal — like means to achieve it. Impure means result in an impure end. Hence the prince and the peasant will not be equalised by cutting off the prince's head, nor can the process of cutting off equalise the employer and employed. One cannot reach truth by untruthfulness".[49]

Gandhiji believed that God creates only for our needs, and, therefore, we have right to fulfil our needs only. Explaining the real meaning of equal distribution he wrote, "The real implication of equal distribution is that each man shall have the wherewithal to supply all his natural requirements and no more".[50] Gandhiji was very well aware of the differences in needs and so he further explained, "If one man has a weak digestion and requires only a quarter of a pound of flour for his bread and another needs a pound, both should be in a position to satisfy their needs".[51] A socialist society must fulfil at least the basic minimum needs of all the individuals. Gandhiji, therefore, advocated a minimum living wage, that is, a wage that should ensure a reasonably balanced diet, shelter and clothing to all, even those who stand at the last rung of the ladder. The spirit of trusteeship is essential to bring about equal distribution through non-violence. Those who are extra brilliant, talented and skilled, must consider themselves merely as trustees and, therefore, must receive for their best efforts a reward that is sufficient to fulfil their needs only. In 1940, Gandhiji wrote, "Indeed at the root of this doctrine of equal distribution must lie that of the trusteeship of the wealthy for the superfluous wealth possessed by them".[52]

Work: Livelihood and Life

Work besides food is another basic need of human beings. Work is a means to earn one's living, it provides opportunity for the necessary exercise of body, it is a source of self-expression, self-fulfilment and creativity, it is a means of service to fellow-beings leading to the fulfilment of spiritual urge. Work is thus not only a source of livelihood, it is an instrument of betterment of life. It is a means to satisfy physical, intellectual as well as spiritual needs. The principle of economic independence and human dignity requires that all those who want work must be able to find employment. Decent and meaningful work must be provided to all the able-bodied individuals of a society.

Gandhiji had given priority to employment over maximisation of output favouring full employment at any cost. In 1921, he wrote passionately, "We should be ashamed of resting or having a square meal so long as there is one able-bodied man or woman without work or food".[53] 'Full employment' as an end in itself is, therefore, one of the basic goals of Gandhian economics. Job creation is the only solution of the problem of poverty acceptable to Gandhiji, he abhores the idea of giving unemployment benefits and doles to the poor. He writes, "My *ahimsa* would not tolerate the idea of giving a free meal to a healthy person who has not worked for it in some honest way, and if I had the power I would stop every *'sadavrat'* where free meals are given. It has degraded the nation and it has encouraged laziness, idleness, hypocrisy and even crime. Such misplaced charity adds nothing to the wealth of the country, whether material or spiritual, and gives a false sense of meritoriousness to the donor. How nice and wise it would be if the donor were to open institutions where they would give meals under healthy, clean surroundings to men and women who would work for them".[54]

The holistic approach demands that all should have the right to meaningful work and, therefore, each individual in a society must be assured gainful employment. Since the function of work is physical development and spiritual unfoldment of man, the nature of employment should be such that besides ensuring each individual a decent living it should provide opportunity for creative self-expression, and be helpful in sharpening the intellect and enriching the soul. Gandhiji had painfully recognised that modern economic system which concentrates on output maximisation, taking employment to be as secondary, automatically adjusting to the level of expenditure, had led to enforced idleness, alienation and dehumanisation, smothering the creativity and spirit of man. Modern economic life has reduced man to be a mere cog in the wheel where work has become a source of conflict, struggle and strife instead of becoming a means for enhancing cooperation and fellow-feeling. Gandhiji, therefore, suggested far reaching changes in the economic structure, methods of production and organisation of economic life and relations, so that work really becomes worship and leads to true happiness and development of man.

Mahatma Gandhi enunciated the principle of bread labour to specify the nature of work that must be done in order to earn one's food. According to the principle of bread labour, each individual must earn his bread by labouring with his own hands. Man deserves food only after having done physical labour. In answer to the question why bread should not be earned by intellectual labour, Gandhiji said, "The needs of the body must be supplied by the body. 'Render into Caesar that which is Caesars', perhaps applies here well".[55] He further added "Mere mental, that is, intellectual labour is for the soul and is its own satisfaction. It should never demand payment. In the ideal state, doctors, lawyers and the like will work solely for the benefit of society, not for self".[56]

Since man has a lot of capacity for work, physical as well as intellectual, after labouring enough for the minimum requirements of food the rest of human faculties should be utilised for the service of mankind. Explaining the full meaning of bread labour, Gandhiji wrote, "The idea is that every healthy individual must labour enough for the food and his intellectual faculties must be exercised not in order to obtain a living or amass a fortune but only in the service of mankind".[57]

Gandhiji specified tilling the soil as the ideal form of bread-labour, however, he had mentioned other occupations also in this regard. "This labour can truly be related to agriculture alone. But at present at any rate, everybody is not in a position to take to it. A person can, therefore, spin or weave, or take up carpentry or smithery, instead of tilling the soil, always regarding agriculture however, to be the ideal".[58]

Gandhiji was inspired by T.M. Bondaref, Tolstoy and Ruskin in arriving at the principle of bread labour. He has quoted the *Bible* and the *Gita* in support of this principle which he has referred to as "divine law". 'In the sweat of thy brow shalt thou eat thy bread',[59] says the *Bible*. Interpreting the 13th and 14th verse in the third chapter of the *Gita*, Gandhiji concludes, "Labouring enough for one's food has been classed in the *Gita* as a *yajna*".[60] The *Gita* further says that whoever eats food without performing *yajna* is a thief. Gandhiji, therefore, asserts that everybody, whether rich or poor, wealth-wise as well as intellect-wise, has a right to eat food only after doing hard physical labour.

It is only voluntary physical labour which can be termed as bread labour and prove a fruitful exercise. Labour done out of compulsion is a state of slavery. As explained by Gandhiji, "Compulsory obedience to a master is a state of slavery, willing obedience to one's father is the glory of the sonship. Similarly, compulsory obedience to the law of bread labour breeds poverty, disease and discontent. It is a state of slavery. Willing obedience to it must bring contentment and health".[61]

Bread labour, which is performed with a definite social purpose behind it, is the highest form of service. Gandhiji has called this voluntary and socially useful labour as 'intelligent' bread labour. He explains, "The adjective 'intelligent' has been prefixed to 'labour' in order to show that labour to be social service must have that definite purpose behind it. Otherwise every labourer can be said to render social service. He does in a way, but what is meant here is something much more than that. A person who labours for the general good of all serves society and is worthy of his hire. Therefore, such bread labour is not different from social service".[62] Willing obedience to the law of bread labour would bring about health and happiness, establish dignity of labour, act as a great equaliser, redress many social and economic evils and bestow upon mankind a number of social and economic benefits. Gandhiji maintains that physical labour "will serve to improve even the quality of his (man's) intellectual output".[63] Further, throwing light on the benefits of bread labour, he has said, "if all laboured for their bread and no more, then there would be enough food and enough leisure for all. Then there would be no cry of over-population, no disease and no such misery as we see around. Such labour will be the highest form of sacrifice".[64]

Integrated Growth

Growth is an ascent of consciousness rooted in the fragment, the relative realm of matter to the consciousness rooted in the whole, the absolute, the Truth. Since man is a being, physical as well as spiritual, and the physical is instrumental in unfolding the spiritual, growth is a function of material as well as moral factors. The meaning of growth in Gandhian economics is good health, bright mind and spiritual richness. As Gandhiji had said, "The end to be sought, is human happiness combined with full mental and material growth. I use the adjective moral synonymous with spiritual".[65] However, the material and the moral influence each other and, therefore, the doctrine of economic growth cannot be viewed independently of spiritual growth and *vice versa*.

Gandhian economics, therefore, suggests a concept of 'integrated growth', comprising of a harmonious integration of both the spiritual as well as material growth. The outer material growth has to be a proper match to the inner spiritual growth. The material growth should never go against the spiritual growth. The material growth, should, however, never fall below the lower limit of providing the minimum physical needs of all the individuals of a society. Furthermore, the parameters of the material growth keep changing according to the understanding of the Truth or the level of inner growth. In other words, economic growth is linked with the level of social consciousness, once the minimum needs of the society have been satisfied.

NOTES

1. Mark Lutz, *Essays in Gandhian Economics*, ed. Ramesh Diwan & Mark Lutz, New Delhi, Gandhi Peace Foundation, 1985, p. 44.
2. *Harijan*, Oct. 13, 1946, *Service Before Self*, ed. Anand T. Hingorani, Bombay, Bhartiya Vidya Bhavan, 1971, p. 76.
3. Ibid., p. 76.
4. *Young India*, Sept. 3, 1925, *CWMG*, Vol. 28, 1968, p. 148.
5. Ibid., Oct. 13, 1921, *CWMG*, Vol. 21, 1966, p. 290.
6. *Harijan*, Oct. 9, 1937, *Selection from Gandhi*, N.K. Bose, Ahmedabad, Navajivan Publishing House, 1948, p. 39.
7. *Young India*, Dec. 26, 1924, *Selection from Gandhi*, Ibid., p. 39.
8. M.K. Gandhi, *Hind Swaraj*, Ahmedabad, Navajivan Publishing House, 1938, p. 65.
9. A.M. Huq, *Welfare Criteria in Gandhian Economics, Essays in Gandhian Economics*, op. cit., p. 72.
10. D.G. Tendulkar, *Mahatma*, Vol. 1, New Delhi, Publications Division, Govt. of India, 1951, p. 108.
11. Romesh Diwan & Mark Lutz, *Essays in Gandhian Economics*, op. cit., p. 13.
12. *CWMG*, Vol. 13, 1964, p. 311.
13. Ibid., p. 314.
14. M.K. Gandhi, *Hind Swaraj*, op. cit., p. 61.
15. Ibid., p. 36.
16. Ibid., p. 37.
17. Ibid.
18. M.K. Gandhi, *Hind Swaraj*, op. cit., p. 63.
19. M.K. Gandhi, *From Yeravda Mandir*, Ahmedabad, Navajivan Publishing House, 1932, p. 5.
20. Quoted in Shanti S. Gupta, *The Economic Philosophy of Mahatma Gandhi*, Delhi, Ashok Publishing House, p. 60.
21. Ibid., p. 60.
22. M.K. Gandhi, *Voluntary Poverty*, comp. Ravindra Kelekar, Ahmedabad, Navajivan Publishing House, 1961, p. 15.
23. Ibid., pp. 14-15.
24. M.K. Gandhi, *From Yeravda Mandir*, op. cit., p. 14.
25. Ibid., p. 16.
26. Ibid., p. 15.
27. M.K. Gandhi, *Voluntary Poverty*, op. cit., p. 4.
28. M.K. Gandhi, *Economic and Industrial Life and Relations*, Vol. I, comp. V.B. Kher, Ahmedabad, Navajivan Publishing House, 1957, p. 160.
29. M.K. Gandhi, *Ashram Observances in Action*, Ahmedabad, Navajivan Publishing House, 1959, p. 113.
30. *Harijan*, June 3, 1939, *Economic and Industrial Life and Relations*, Vol. 1, op. cit., p. 157.
31. *Harijan*, Jan. 30, 1937, *CWMG*, Vol. 64, 1976, p. 264.
32. M.K. Gandhi, *Yeravda Mandir*, op. cit., p. 17.
33. *Voluntary Poverty*, op. cit., p. 5.
34. M.K. Gandhi, *Hind Swaraj*, op. cit., p. 61.
35. *Harijan*, Aug. 29, 1936, *CWMG*, Vol. 63, 1976, p. 241.

36. *Young India*, Oct. 27, 1921, *CWMG*, Vol. 21, 1966, p. 357.
37. *CWMG*, Vol. 13, 1964, p. 219.
38. *Harijan*, Jan. 18, 1949, *Sarvodaya*, ed. Bharatan Kumarappa, Ahmedabad, Navajivan Publishing House, 1954, p. 5.
39. John Ruskin, *Unto This Last*, London, George Allen and Unwin Ltd., 1960, pp. 64-65.
40. M.K. Gandhi, *An Autobiography or the Story of My Experiments with Truth*, Ahmedabad, Navajivan Publishing House, 1927, p. 224.
41. *Young India*, Mar. 26, 1931, *India of My Dreams*, comp. R.K. Prabhu, Ahmedabad, Navajivan Publishing House, 1947, p. 9.
42. Ibid., Oct. 15, 1931, *Ibid.*, p. 53.
43. Ibid., Nov. 15, 1928, Ibid., pp. 70-71.
44. *The Message of Mahatma Gandhi*, op. cit., p. 87.
45. Romesh Diwan & Mark Lutz, *Essays in Gandhian Economics*, op. cit., p. 60.
46. *Harijan*, July 13, 1947, M.K. Gandhi, *Towards Non-Violent Socialism*, ed. Bharatan Kumarappa, Ahmedabad, Navajivan Publishing House, 1951, p. 9.
47. *Harijan*, Jan. 15, 1938, *CWMG*, Vol. 66, 1976, p. 341.
48. M.K. Gandhi, *Constructive Programme*, Ahmedabad, Navajivan Publishing House, 1941, p. 25.
49. *Harijan*, July 13, 1947, *Towards Non-Violent Socialism*, op. cit., p. 10.
50. *Harijan*, Aug. 25, 1940, *CWMG*, Vol. 72, 1978, p. 399.
51. Ibid.
52. Ibid., p. 400.
53. *Young India*, Oct. 6, 1921, *India of My Dreams*, op. cit., p. 47.
54. *Young India*, Aug. 13, 1925, *CWMG*, Vol. 28, 1968, p. 60.
55. *Harijan*, June 29, 1935, *CWMG*, Vol. 61, 1975, p. 212.
56. Ibid., p. 212.
57. M.K. Gandhi, *Economic and Industrial Life and Relations*, op. cit., p. 105.
58. M.K. Gandhi, *Yeravda Mandir*, op. cit., p. 24.
59. Ibid., p. 23.
60. M.K. Gandhi, *Economic and Industrial Life and Relations*, op. cit., p. 106.
61. *Harijan*, June 29, 1935, *CWMG*, Vol. 61, 1975, p. 212.
62. Ibid., June 1, 1935, Ibid., Vol. 61, 1975, p. 126.
63. Ibid., Feb. 23, 1947, *Towards Non-Violent Socialism*, op. cit., p. 18.
64. Ibid., June 29, 1935, *CWMG*, Vol. 61, 1975, pp. 211-212.
65. Ibid., Jan. 18, 1942, Ibid., Vol. 75, 1979, p. 216.

6

THE HOLISTIC MEANS

THE HOLISTIC paradigm takes ends and means to be the two sides of the same coin in contrast to the fragmentary world-view which separates them and, therefore, justifies the achievement of ends by any means. According to Gandhian philosophy, means and ends are convertible terms, the achievement of ends is in direct proportion to the nature of means adopted. As Gandhiji has expressed, "They say 'means are after all means', I would say 'means are after all everything'. As the means so the end. There is no wall of separation between means and end. Indeed, the Creator has given us control (and that too very limited) over means, none over the end. Realisation of the goal is in exact proportion to that of the means. This is a proposition that admits of no exception".[1] Ends are the outcome of the means and so Gandhiji wrote, "The means may be likened to a seed, the end to a tree; and there is just the same inviolable connection between the means and the end as there is between the seed and the tree".[2]

Truth is the end and non-violence, that is action arising out of truth, is the means to realise it. Violent means embedded in untruth will ultimately lead to violence only. Truth cannot be realised by untruth. Gandhi, therefore, pronounced "Truthful conduct alone can reach truth".[3]

Economic ends which are centred in truth must also be achieved only by non-violent, truthful means. The truth of the wholeness of life must not be violated in any way. Gandhian economic philosophy, therefore, emphasises the achievement of economic ends by holistic means. Policies and methods devised to achieve the truthful economic ends must never become an instrument of violence against nature, man and society, the various elements of the holistic plan. The means adopted to achieve the economic ends have, thus, constraints not only economic but also holistic. Truth, Non-violence, Equality, Non-exploitation, *Swadeshi*, Trusteeship and Freedom for total development and unfoldment of human personality, are, therefore, the basic moral values underlying the means to achieve the desired economic ends setforth in Chapter 5.

The existing economic system, Neo-classical as well as the Marxian, which may be termed as systems of violence, being based on a fragmentary paradigm, have led to an irrepressible economic crisis of a complex and global nature. Gandhian economic system comprising of a holistic economic structure and non-violent methods of production and distribution not only proposes to mitigate the evils of the present economic order but also assures man a decent standard of living as well as moral elevation. Regarding the twin objectives of Gandhian plans, the spiritual and the economic, Bharatan Kumarappa has remarked, "While his plans for village reconstruction are motivated by a passionate desire to ameliorate hunger and want in the villages, they are also prompted by an equally earnest zeal for spiritual ends such as non-violence, peace, social justice and freedom in the sense of self-dependence and self-reliance even for the lowliest and the lost".[4]

Decentralisation, Self-Sufficiency, and Swadeshi

Decentralisation and self-sufficiency are the basic economic principles underlying Gandhian non-violent economic structure and methods. To Gandhiji, man is of supreme consideration. Each individual has unlimited potentiality and, therefore, each individual must find full opportunity for self-expression, and fulfilment of personality. Centralisation smothers the spirit of man and kills the individual initiative and creativity. In a non-violent economic system, economic power is to be decentralised and lodged in small economic units so that, ultimately, the individual as a consumer, producer, or worker may have the freedom to take economic decisions and also become an effective participant in the planned development of an economy. Freedom or *Swaraj* in Gandhian terminology is, however, not liberty without responsibility. The individual is to exercise his freedom in the light of Truth of his existence, fully realising that he is an integral part of a whole. The liberty of the individual is not to be exercised against the liberty of the other constituent parts of the holistic plan. Explaining the meaning of *Swaraj*, Gandhiji wrote, "The root meaning of *swaraj* is self-rule. *Swaraj* may, therefore, be rendered as disciplined rule from within. . . . Independence may mean licence to do as you like. . . . *Swaraj* is positive, Independence is negative. . . The word *'Swaraj'* is a sacred word, a vedic word, meaning self-rule and self-restraint and not freedom from all restraints which 'independence' often means".[5] As interpreted by G. Thimmaiah, Gandhian view of decentralisation, therefore, means, "Voluntarily giving responsibility to the people to make decisions of their own affairs, subject to certain broad guidelines, which would not conflict with the overall framework of the society".[6]

Centralisation of power political or economic, is the source of all kinds of exploitation resulting in curtailment of individual liberty, regimentation of the masses, unemployment, and poverty. Decentralisation, on the other hand, counters all exploitation, restores human freedom and dignity and promotes human values like fellow feeling and cooperation, sanctity of labour and simplicity, thus elevating the moral fibre of man. As remarked by Shriman Narayan, Violence logically leads to centralisation; the essence of non-violence is decentralisation".[7] In Gandhiji's words, "The end to be sought is human happiness combined with full mental and moral growth. I use the adjective moral as synonymous with spiritual. This end can be achieved under decentralisation. Centralisation as a system is inconsistent with non-violent structure of society".[8]

Self-sufficiency besides decentralisation, is another condition of a non-violent economic order. Mahatma Gandhi envisioned the organisation of economic life in India as composed of a number of decentralised self-sufficient economic units. He chose the village to be the basic operational unit in India to be developed along the lines of decentralisation and self-sufficiency. "Independence must begin at the bottom, thus every village will be a republic or panchayat having full powers",[9] he asserted. As a matter of fact, self-reliance was advocated by Gandhiji as a basic principle of life because dependence brings in exploitation which is the essence of violence. The poor is exploited by the rich, the village by the city and the under-developed country by the developed ones due to lack of self-sufficiency. The British shattered our rural economy through competition, exploited the villages, and forced the people to live in sub-human conditions. Gandhiji emphasised reorganisation of economic life on the lines of decentralisation and self-sufficiency in order to counter all exploitation whether by the capitalist, by the city or by the rich developed economies. "Rural economy as I have conceived it eschews exploitation and exploitation is the essence of violence",[10] said he. Besides providing freedom from exploitation, self-sufficiency leads to fuller development and unfoldment of human personality. The self-sufficient communities learn how to grow in cooperation as well as experience a glow of freedom.

Swadeshi is the basic moral principle underlying a decentralised, self-sufficient economic structure. According to the definition given by Mahatma Gandhi, "*Swadeshi* is that spirit in us which restricts us to the use and service of our immediate surroundings to the exclusion of the more remote".[11] Man's physical capacity to serve being limited, he has to make a choice regarding the field of service. Man's first duty is towards his family, village and region which has been made his first care by nature. This is '*Swadharma*' as given in the *Gita*, applied to one's immediate environment. If everyone followed the principle of *Swadeshi*, there would be no one in the world unloved and unattended. *Swadeshi* must never be taken to mean selfishness; rather in its purest sense, it is the acme of universal service. As Gandhiji maintains, "*Swadeshi* is the only doctrine consistent with the law of humility and love. It is arrogance to think of launching out to serve the whole of India when I am hardly able to serve even my own family. It were better to concentrate my effort upon the family and consider that through them I was serving the whole of nation and, if you will the whole of humanity. This is humility and it is love".[12]

In economic terms, a strict adherence to the *Swadeshi* doctrine paves the way to a decentralised, self-sufficient economy. The buyers and sellers having a concern for each other, jointly work for the development of their local area using local resources. Imbued with a spirit of *Swadeshi*, if people devote their energies for the betterment of the region to which they belong, "Then", Gandhiji concluded, "every village of India will almost be a self-supporting and self-contained unit exchanging only such necessary commodities with other villages where they are not locally producible".[13]

Structure of a Non-Violent Economy

Based on the principles of decentralisation, self-sufficiency, the spirit of *Swadeshi* and cooperation, Gandhiji spent a lot of his time in working out the details of a non-violent economic structure which was one of the main aspects of his constructive programme. The structure of a non-violent economy is composed of a number of decentralised self-sufficient economic units. The size of the units varies according to the geographical, economic and social factors of a region. In India, Gandhiji chose the village to be the basic economic unit. Defining it on the basis of population, he said, "My imaginary Village consists of

1,000 souls. Such a unit can give good account of itself, if it is well organised on a basis of self-sufficiency".[14]

To counter exploitation of all kinds, the village must be self-reliant in the supply of all its necessities, producing sufficiently enough for supporting all its inhabitants at a decent standard of living. In other words, all local requirements like supplies of food, vegetable, fruit, agriculture and industrial products, local communications, transport, fuel, housing, etc., should be fulfilled by the people themselves within the framework of their economic unit. Village self-sufficiency, however, does not mean denial of sharing and cooperation wherever required. As Gandhiji wrote in *Harijan* in 1942, "My idea of village *swaraj* is that it is a complete republic independent of its neighbours for its own vital wants, and yet dependent for many others in which dependence is a necessity".[15]

Gandhiji's main idea on the basic framework of a self-sufficient village economy may be summed up as follows:

(i) Every village will grow for its own food, crops and cotton for its cloth.
(ii) It will have a land reserve for grazing its cattle, recreation and playground for children.
(iii) If there is more land available, it will grow useful money crops, excluding ganja, tobacco, opium and the like.
(iv) It will maintain a village theatre, school and public hall and houses of worship for all.
(v) It will have its own waterworks, ensuring clean water supply. This can be done through wells or tanks.
(vi) Education will be compulsory up to the final basic course.
(vii) The village will be so constructed as to lend itself to proper sanitation. It will have cottages with proper light and ventilation.
(viii) Economic resources obtainable in the nearby surroundings will be used as far as possible.
(ix) Basic medical facilities will be made available in the village.
(x) Economic activities will be organised on a cooperative basis as far as possible.

It was Gandhiji's firm conviction that village economy organised on the basis of decentralisation and self-sufficiency will lead to a happy, healthy and meaningful life leading to a harmonious development and total unfoldment of human personality. "When our villages are fully developed there will be no dearth in them of men with a high degree of skill and artistic talent. There will be village poets, village artists, village architects, linguists and research workers. In short, there will be nothing in life worth having which will not be had in the villages. Today the villages are dung heaps. Tomorrow they will be like tiny gardens of Eden where dwell highly intelligent folk whom no one can deceive or exploit",[16] he had envisioned.

Gandhian economic units have a degree of specialisation according to the natural skill, talent, aptitude and capabilities of its inhabitants. However, the extent of the market is limited to the village only as far as possible. Prices are determined by the mutual cooperation and agreement of the buyers and sellers. The driving force of the producers and consumers is not maximisation of profits and utility but maximisation of social welfare.

The spirit of *Swadeshi*, guiding man's economic behaviour, leads to natural love and preference for local products and an attitude of service to the immediate neighbours. The consumers for their requirements must buy from the local producers and thus support the local farmers, artisans such as weavers, carpenters, cobblers and potters etc. Adherence to the principle of *Swadeshi* leads to a natural economic order and harmony. Gandhiji was of the confirmed view that the breach of the sacred law of *Swadeshi* had led to poverty, unemployment, pauperism and degradation of economic life in India. In an address at the Missionary Conference, Madras, he had said, "Much of the deep poverty of the masses is due to the ruinous departure from *Swadeshi* in the economic and industrial life. If not an article of commerce had been brought from outside India, she would be today a land flowing with milk and honey".[17] Gandhiji, therefore, gave a call to the people to take up the vow of *Swadeshi*. A *Swadeshi* mentality requires a determination to buy everything from the local producers, even if their goods are costlier and qualitatively inferior to the goods produced by outsiders. Not only that the consumers should buy from the local manufacturers, they should help them in bringing about improvement wherever required. As explained by Gandhiji, "A votary of *Swadeshi* will carefully study his environment and try to help his neighbours, wherever possible by giving preference to local manufacturers, even if they are of an inferior grade or dearer in price than things manufactured elsewhere. He will try to remove their defects, but will not, because of their defects give them up in favour of foreign manufactures".[18] Producers on their part must take up a cooperative attitude towards the poor customers, and also do their best in order to satisfy the individual requirements. The cooperation between consumers and producers will lead to a downward shift of the cost curve and an upward shift of the revenue curve so that the production of many commodities needed by the consumers will become viable in the village only. The process, if continued, will lead to the decentralised economic units becoming self-sufficient in all respects.

The decentralised economic units would, thus, facilitate the best possible use of local raw materials, talents and manpower, promote occupational equilibrium, ecological balance and cooperative living. The village would be able to produce whatever is required with the help of local resources and would be contented with whatever has been produced in closer surroundings. Mutual help, cooperation and sharing among the various economic units is, however, not ruled out. Exchange will take place for necessaries which are not producible within the individual unit and help and cooperation will be rendered wherever needed. Exploitation, coercion and violence in any corner is, however, absent. The individual though conscious of its being a part of the whole, stands in its own dignity and splendour. The essence of the individual and collective life in a non-violent economic order has been aptly summed up by Gandhiji in the following passage:

> "In this structure composed of innumerable villages there will be ever widening, never ascending circles. Life will not be a pyramid with the apex sustained by the bottom. But it will be an oceanic circle whose centre will be the individual, always ready to perish for the village, the latter ready to perish for the circle of villages, till at last the whole becomes one life composed of individuals, never aggressive in their arrogance but ever humble, sharing the majesty of the oceanic circle of which they are integral units. Therefore, the outmost circumference will not wield power to crush the inner circle but give strength to all within and derive its own from the centre".[19]

Promotion of Khadi and Village Industries

Industrialisation on a mass scale necessarily leads to the passive or active exploitation of the village. Large scale unemployment and poverty take place due to centralisation and monopolistic tendencies, the rich get richer and the gains of industrialisation hardly percolate down to the poor sections of society. As a matter of fact, craze for industrialisation has led to the destruction of our rural industries and has ruined the self-sufficient character of the village economy.

Gandhiji ardently advocated the revival and promotion of Khadi and Village Industries in India as he felt that this alone would help the dumb millions. He gave *'charkha'* the highest place of honour, considering it to be hope of the masses capable of winning *'Purna Swaraj'*. Development of Khadi industries leads to the development of many other anterior and posterior industries like ginning, carding, warping, dyeing and weaving. Gandhiji rightly remarked, "Khadi is the sun of the village solar system. The planets are the various industries which can support Khadi in return for the heat and sustenance they derive from it".[20] Besides Khadi, there are industries like hand grinding, hand pounding, soap making, paper making, match making, tanning, oil-pressing etc. which can be developed and utilised for the development of the village.

The prime consideration in encouraging the village and cottage industries is the concern for the problem of poverty and unemployment. Gandhiji was painfully hurt by the criminal neglect of the peasants and artisans of India which had reduced them to pauperism, dullness and habitual illness. Promotion of village industries which can be carried out without creating heavy demands on capital, he felt, would immediately drive starvation and poverty from this country and "put millions of rupees into the pockets of the villagers".[21] A policy of decentralisation and modernisation of rural industries would provide immediate solution to the problem of open unemployment and disguised unemployment, remove poverty, inequalities and exploitation. "No country in the world can prosper that has one-third of time of the vast majority of the inhabitants lying unutilised",[22] warned Gandhiji. Revival and encouragement of village industries would create opportunity for self-employment and make man not only independent but also provide him freedom for creativity and expression. It may be argued that the development of small-scale, labour intensive, village industries will hamper the generation of surplus and hence retard economic growth. However, the pattern of industrial development suggested by Gandhiji is fairly justified in the light of the fact that the purpose of Gandhian holistic economics is not maximisation of production but optimisation of production ensuring fulfilment of basic needs and gainful employment to all the individuals with dignity and independence.

An essential condition for the successful implementation of a programme of rural industrialisation is the spirit of *Swadeshi.* There has to be a strong determination on the part of the people to find all their necessaries produced in the villages. Gandhiji felt that there is hardly anything of daily use which the villagers have not made before and which they cannot make now. The consumers must make a conscious effort to substitute village products for those produced in the city. He suggested, "We begin with ourselves and thus use, say hand made paper instead of mill made, use village reed, where possible instead of the fountain-pen or the penholder, ink made in the village instead of the big factories etc."[23] Khadi, vitamin laden, nourishing gud or molasses and unpolished rice are some of the major village products that could be used instead of the products of big textile, sugar and rice mills. The duty of those imbued with a spirit of *Swadeshi* lies in investigating the possibility of keeping in existence the village wheel, the village crushers and the village pounder by advertising their products, discovering their qualities, ascertaining the condition of the workers and the number displaced by the power-driven machinery and discovering the methods of improving them, whilst retaining their village character. *Swadeshi*, according to Gandhiji is the key to the economic salvation of India. So, he reflected, "Those who think deep will see that such swadeshi contains pure economics. Imitation of English economics will spell our ruin".[24]

Suitable economic measures on the part of the Government will be needed for the revival and promotion of village industries and also for protecting this sector from competition from big industries until it becomes economically viable. People will have to transform their attitude and organise themselves in order to help the village industries. All India Spinners Association and All India Village Industries Association formed under the guidance of Gandhiji have made very useful contribution in this regard.

Machinery, Capital Intensity and Scale of Production

The process of industrialisation in modern economics is accompanied by technological progress leading to capital intensive large-scale production. The purpose of industrial advancement is maximisation of consumption now or in future. However, economic growth attributed to industrialisation of this nature is not without its ill effects. Large scale, capital intensive, mechanised production ultimately adversely affects the life of man, his relationships and the environment in which he lives. Gandhiji who advocated optimum level of consumption took serious view of the ill effects of industrialisation. He has spoken and written at length on the evils of machinery and industrialisation. In 'Hind Swaraj', he said, "Machinery is like a snake-hole which may contain from one to hundred snakes".[25] However, he never expressed unqualified opposition to machinery and industrialisation. He favoured machinery within limits and advocated labour intensive small scale industries, village handicrafts and cottage industries. He also did not completely rule out the large-scale, heavy, capital intensive industries in the national interest, provided they be kept strictly under public control.

Technology or 'Machinery' in Gandhian terminology used for the purpose of unlimited economic growth leads to the fast depletion of the non-renewable world resources, pollution and problems of ecology. There are limits to which the natural process can replenish them. As discussed in Chapter 3, nature cannot cope up with unlimited industrialisation and technological advancement; the process if unchecked will ultimately lead to the collapse of the world economic system. According to Schumacher, "Modern industrial system with all its intellectual sophistication, consumes the very basis on which it has been erected".[26] Gandhian Holistic Economics suggests an economy of permanence. Industrialisation and technological progress must be carried out within limits so that the natural processes are not disturbed. Non-renewable resources must not be wrecklessly wasted. They must be used only if they are indispensable. An economy of permanence requires that we must return to nature what we receive from her. Not only that industrialisation and technology must be within limits, the scale of operations must also be small. Advocating small-scale operations, Schumacher has said, "Small-scale operations, no matter how numerous, are always less likely to be harmful to the natural environment than large-scale ones, simply because their individual force is small in relation to the recuperative forces of nature".[27]

Machinery leads to human debasement physically, mentally and morally. The baneful influence of machinery on man has been recognised by Adam Smith, David Ricardo, Karl Marx and other noted economists. It kills initiative, freedom and creativity of the individual. Men are turned into machine minders with little freedom to exercise their own creative faculties. The big organisation due to the large-scale application of technology leading to urbanisation, alienates man from nature, his fellow beings, work and his product. Work becomes completely joyless and, therefore, in their leisure hours the workers simply become passive consumers of mechanised goods and entertainment. Schumacher, who advocated appropriate technology or technology with a human face, has remarked. "Modern technology has deprived man of the kind of work that he enjoys most, creative useful work with hands and brains and given him plenty of work of fragmented kind most of which he does not enjoy at all".[28] The application of large-scale technology to industry has either turned man into an exploiter giving full vent to selfishness, envy and violence lying dormant within him or has led him to become the exploited, always living in fear, insecurity, depression and frustration. According to Gandhiji, development of science and technology without spiritual advancement always leads to dehumanisation of man, degradation and destruction. He, therefore, advocated limits to be imposed on machinery, favouring small-scale production and organisation of life in small communities so that the essential human link between man and nature, his work and product, employer and the employed, producer and consumer is not broken. Modern sociology also upholds the principle that man is happiest when living in small communities.

Gandhian principle of bread labour also requires that machinery must be kept within limits. Everybody must do some physical labour to deserve the food that one eats in order to maintain the body. This is the sacred law expounded in the *Gita* and the *Bible*. The breach of the principle amounts to theft according to the *Gita*, "If one eats fruits of the earth, rendering to kindly Heaven no gift of toil that thief steals from his world".[29] If this sacred law of bread labour is followed by all, the use of machinery would automatically fall within its proper limits.

Excessive use of machinery leads to decay of human body due to lack of proper use and required exercise. Gandhiji observed, "We are destroying the matchless living machines, viz., our own bodies, by leaving them to rust and trying to substitute lifeless machinery for them".[30]

As technological innovations take place with the advance of industrialisation, wealth gets concentrated in the hands of a few, sharp inequalities of income accrue, and society gets sharply polarised giving rise to a dualistic nature of economy. The concentration of economic power becomes a cumulative process like a snowball gathering more and more snow, due to more and more technological innovations. The process feeds upon exploitation, the 'haves' exploiting the 'have-nots' at various levels of life. Gandhiji's holistic outlook sharply noticed that machinery leads to the exploitation of the poor by the rich, the employed by the employer, labour by capital, village by the city. At the international level, the developed countries exploit the under-developed countries. The so-called transfer of technology from developed countries to under-developed countries these days has also become a source of exploitation. The rich countries dump their obsolete and harmful technologies in the poor countries. These technologies make the rich more rich and the poor, poorer.

Professor Galbraith in his writings has laid bare the exploitation carried out by the giant business corporations arising as a result of modern industrial system. He has held that they tend to reduce the state to a subservient position. They exploit the third world countries, control the media, the education system, and the market through advertisements and propaganda, ultimately proving that it is the producer who is the sovereign and not the consumer. Reacting sharply to the evils of machinery, Gandhiji said, "I will not have the enrichment of a few at the expense of the community. At present, the machine is helping a small minority to live on the exploitation of the masses".[31] He further positively asserted, "I want the concentration of wealth, not in the hands of a few, but in the hands of all. Today machinery merely helps a few to ride on the backs of millions".[32]

The views of economists like Schumpeter, Joan Robinson and Marx bear close similarity to those of Gandhiji's as far as the evils of technology are concerned. Innovations and technological progress lead to monopolistic exploitation, unemployment and a capitalist class thriving upon 'surplus value' arising from the exploitation of labour. As Marx sharply commented on the process of industrialisation, "Along with the constantly diminishing number of the magnets of capital, who usurp and monopolise all advantages of this process of transformation, grows the mass of misery, oppression, slavery, degradation, exploitation".[33] Gandhiji who considered exploitation to be the essence of all violence, therefore, emphatically declared, "I am a determined foe of all machinery that is designed for exploitation of people".[34] On being questioned whether he was opposed to machinery only because and when it concentrated production and distribution in the hands of the few, he had pointedly replied, "Whatever cannot be shared with the masses is taboo to me".[35]

Gandhiji's central point of opposition to machinery was that in a country abundant with labour, machinery inevitably leads to unemployment. According to modern economics, the use of technology is warranted because it saves labour and hence helps in the reduction of cost. Displacement of labour is labour saving in an economy having shortage of labour; however in an economy where labour is abundant, displacement of labour swells the rank of the unemployed. Gandhiji for whom full employment was one of the major goals of a non-violent economy, therefore, argued, "Mechanisation is good when the hands are too few for the work intended to be accomplished. It is an evil when there are more hands than required for the work, as is the case in India. . . . The problem with us is not how to find leisure for the teeming millions inhabiting our villages. The problem is how to utilise their idle hours, which are equal to the working days of six months in the year".[36] Criticising the craze for machinery which is introduced in the name of labour saving but which eventually leads to unemployment, Gandhiji commented, "Men go on 'saving labour' till thousands are without work and thrown on the open streets to die of starvation. I want to save time and labour not for a fraction of mankind, but for all".[37] Gandhiji was profoundly moved when he saw that machinery creates unemployment, leading to poverty, malnutrition, starvation, hunger and death; he, therefore,wrote poignantly, "Dead machinery must not be pitted against the millions of living machines".[38]

Modern economics favours capital intensive techniques from the point of view of 'rate of surplus criterion' so that the total output may be maximised on some future date. However, as the process of industrialisation begins in an under-developed economy, the modern sector in the urban areas thrives but the traditional sector in the rural areas decays. The traditional handicrafts and village small-scale industries which are labour intensive in nature perish because they are unable to stand the competition from the large-scale capital-intensive industries. As the village small-scale industries decay, self-employed workers are uprooted and forced idleness is created leading to unemployment and poverty. As Gandhiji has observed, "We are seeing the process going on before our eyes, little flour mills are ousting the *chakkis*, oil mills the village *ghani*, rice mills the village *dhenkis*, sugarmills the village gur-pans etc. This displacement of village labour is impoverishing the villagers and enriching the moneyed men".[39] To describe the process in the words of B.N. Ganguli, "Indeed, what

Myrdal calls the 'backwash' effects of development in urban pockets would tend to denude the countryside of its skill and vitality, leaving the rest to stagnate more and face worse conditions of unemployment and privation".[40]

As the rural areas are impoverished, a second phase of decay in the traditional sector ensues. Since there is poverty there is shortage of purchasing power and, therefore, the village industries are further ruined because of a lack of market for their products. The capital resources from all over the country are drawn to the large industries where there are high profits, and have a tendency to shy away from the small-scale industries which have become relatively quite unprofitable. Even the vital raw materials needed by them are sucked away by large enterprises. The efforts of the state at planned economic development generally go to the benefit of big industrialists in a mixed capitalistic enterprise system. A policy of large public spending results in the cumulative rise of prices, which further complicates the situation. The entire process thus entails impoverishment of the masses, widespread unemployment, mass migration to metropolitan centres, on the one hand, and concentration of economic power, income and wealth leading to conspicuous consumption of sophisticated goods, malallocation of scarce economic resources and balance of payment difficulties, on the other.

The Keynesian solution of raising the level of investment to generate the necessary 'effective demand' in order to cure the problem of unemployment is not applicable in the under-developed economies which suffer from structural unemployment. The poor economies suffer from a lack of investible resources. Moreover, investment in an under-developed economy creates inflation through the 'multiplier effect' instead of creating employment and increasing real income. This is because of the presence of various bottlenecks and lags and absence of necessary capital in the economy. Furthermore, the scope of profitable investment is narrowed due to a general lack of purchasing power to buy the consumption goods which the capital goods help to produce. In under-developed economies, there is the problem of lack of capital as well as lack of effective demand, the simultaneous existence of which gives rise to a vicious circle of poverty and unemployment.

The efforts to accelerate the rate of investment by investing in the surplus generating, capital intensive industries, ultimately, lead to a situation when there is overcapacity built-up in capital goods industries and a vast reservoir of poverty and unemployment in the rural areas. In the words of Amritananda Das, "The capital goods capacity is being built up for an industrial system which is not there. The economy, then, comes to a point at which there is a large capital goods industry capacity left facing a sea of rural poverty".[41] To quote him further, "The rural sector cannot absorb 'capital goods'.The consumer goods sector cannot expand because there are no adequate 'markets', with the vast majority of the work-force locked in a backward and poor rural sector".[42] Gandhiji has thus rightly asserted that in a poor country, large-scale industrialisation with indiscriminate technology would ultimately lead to unemployment, poverty, misery and suffering on the part of the masses. "Industrialisation on a mass scale will necessarily lead to passive or active exploitation of the villagers as the problems of competition and marketing come in",[43] he had concluded.

Since unlimited technological progress leads to poverty and unemployment, Gandhiji wanted modernisation to take place within limits. His main aim was 'full employment' and removal of poverty and not the eradication of all machinery. In other words, Gandhiji was advocating labour intensive techniques of production in labour abundant countries like India so that the total working force may be fully employed. "If I could produce all my country's wants by means of 30,000 people instead of 30 million, I should not mind it, provided that the thirty million are not rendered idle and unemployed".[44] In economic terminology, as described by Amritananda. Das, the technological choice must ensure that the incremental employment-capital ratio is not lower than the ratio between the current increment of work-force and the available supply of investible funds.

Though Gandhiji vehemently criticised machinery because of its inherent evils, yet his opposition was not indiscriminate and total. He recognised the good influence of machinery on labour productivity and in reducing the burden of human drudgery. He favoured machinery as far as it helped man without creating its evil influence. On being asked whether he was against all machinery, Gandhiji had answered, "How can I be, when I know that even this body is a most delicate piece of machinery? The spinning wheel itself is a machine; a little toothpick is a machine. What I object to is the craze for machinery, not machinery as such".[45] To Gandhiji man is the supreme consideration. He welcomed machinery so long as it helped in saving individual labour and lightened the burden of man, but he strongly rejected it as soon as it became an instrument of greed and exploitation, killing the freedom and individuality of man. He wanted machines to cater to the needs of man, to serve man, and not to be the master of man. Gandhian non-violent technology thus connotes, 'The saving of labour of the individual should be the object, and honest humanitarian considerations, and not greed, the motive".[46]

Techniques of production in the decentralised, self-sufficient economic sector in a poor country like India would have to be very simple in order to ensure full employment, non-exploitation, freedom and equality, to the masses. Gandhiji, therefore, pleaded for the revival of handicrafts, village and small-scale industries in the traditional sector. The existing local technology must be revived and improved upon. The *'charkha'* received the place of pride and honour only because it symbolises employment, freedom, equality, decentralisation and self-sufficiency. Decentralisation, in a country with shortage of capital, means that the tools have to be simple, cheap, easy to handle and easy to repair.

Gandhiji was, however, willing to accept heavy and large scale industries with high technology in the national interest provided they are under state control and are subservient to the needs of the village and small industries. Gandhiji thus visualised a harmonious integration of industries with different capital intensities. Dr. J.D. Sethi is of the opinion that a full spectrum of technologies would be acceptable under Gandhian economic system, provided they satisfied the basic objectives of a non-violent economy. To quote him, "the Gandhian system includes both the aeroplane and the bullock-cart. In the society of his vision, traditional technologies go through continuous improvement, modification etc., to reduce the burden and drudgery of the working people and help them to produce more, but without creating the enslavement of man".[47]

Distribution Simultaneous with Production

Equality is one of the main principles of a non-violent economy. All that is produced by the world-resources must be shared equally by all. The glaring differences between the classes and the masses and the wide gulf between the rich and the poor is a painful sight and is against all norms of social justice. Gandhiji, therefore, strongly advocated, "the levelling down of the few rich in whose hands is concentrated the bulk of the nation's wealth on the one hand, and the levelling up of the semi-starved naked millions on the other".[48] How can we bring about equality? Non-violent, holistic means would never suggest a bloody revolution. Gandhiji wanted to strike at the roots of the inequalities of income. Centralisation of production leading to concentration of economic power in the hands of a few, is the chief source of inequalities of income and exploitation. Gandhiji, therefore, suggested decentralisation, production by masses instead of mass production so that distribution can take place simultaneously with production. Economic power should be diffused and dispersed so that every worker either becomes self-employed or enjoys joint ownership of some small-scale industry. Now production is in people's own homes and there being no gap between production and distribution, distribution is simultaneous with production. Such a system would surely avoid all inequalities of income and concentration of wealth and economic power.

Mass production leads to the necessity of capturing world markets resulting in accumulation of wealth. Production by masses, on the other hand, is production for local needs. According to Gandhiji distribution can be equalised only when production is localised, it will never be equal so long as there is the desire to tap other markets to dispose of produced goods. Localisation of production is the answer to all our problems regarding distribution. As described by him, "when production and consumption both become localised the temptation to speed up production, indefinitely and at any price, disappears. All the endless difficulties and problems that our present day economic system presents, too, would then come to and end. . . . There would be no unnatural accumulation or hoards in the pockets of the few, and want in the midst of plenty in regard to the rest, as is happening today".[49]

If distribution and production do not take place simultaneously, the equilibrium between demand and supply cannot be brought about easily due to market distortions and, therefore, the economy suffers from booms and slumps. In Gandhiji's words, "Without simultaneous distribution on an equally mass scale, the production can result only in a great world tragedy".[50] When production and distribution go together, the producer directly caters to the needs of the consumer and there are no surpluses and shortages. The distribution costs in a decentralised, self-sufficient economy are reduced to the minimum. The centralised mass production leaves a wide scope for exploitation by the middleman, fraud and speculation. Gandhiji, therefore, is categorical in stating that the mania for mass production is responsible for world crisis. To quote him, "Granting for the moment that the machinery may supply all the needs of humanity, still it would concentrate production for particular areas, so that you would have to go in a round-about way to regulate distribution; whereas, if there is production and distribution both in the respective areas where things are required, it is automatically regulated, and there is less chance for fraud, none for speculation".[51]

International Trade

According to the principle of comparative advantage, the nations of the world must enter into free trade to maximise their economic gains. Gandhian holistic economics rejects the doctrine of the international trade on the basis of the principle of Swadeshi. The rejection follows from the Gandhian definition of human welfare in holistic terms in contrast to that by modern economics in terms of maximisation of consumption goods.

The principle of *Swadeshi*, on spiritual basis, demands that there should be a natural preference for goods produced in our immediate surroundings. "Just as we do not give up our country for one with a better climate but endeavour to improve our own, so also may we not discard Swadeshi for better or cheaper foreign things".[52] It is disloyalty to our country and violation of the principle of *Swadharma* to prefer foreign goods when they are available in our own country or can be made available with a little effort.

Now, purely on economic grounds, trade in the conventional sense among unequal partners, when one country is under-developed and the other is developed, will ultimately harm the interest of the poor country. Import of industrial products leads to the extinction of the handicrafts and the small-scale home industries in the under-developed countries due to their economic inability to stand competition. Consequently, there is a big drain on primary products, raw materials and non-renewable resources in order to meet the demand of the foreign countries. The under-developed country, therefore, gradually becomes more and more impoverished. The natural home economy is shattered without any hope for future. There is large-scale unemployment, and people become poor, degraded and lustreless. The rich country exploits the poor country by offering poor terms of trade and pocketing the major share of the gains. According to J.C. Kumarappa, if any society depends for its necessities on foreign countries, the degree of its exploitation is in direct proportion to the amount of goods imported. Moreover, "Consumption of foreign goods is definitely a bait for the foreigners to occupy the country".[53] He has further suggested that trade should be restricted only to surplus commodities in order to give no occasion to exploitation.

Gandhiji, deeply pained by the process of exploitation due to foreign trade, had expressed, "Economics that permit one country to prey upon another are immoral. It is sinful to buy and use articles made by sweated labour. It is sinful to eat American wheat and let my neighbour, the grain-dealer, starve for want of custom. Similarly, it is sinful for me to wear the latest finery of Regent Street, when I know that if I had but worn the things woven by the neighbouring spinners and weavers, that would have clothed me, and fed and clothed them".[54] Gandhiji was of the confirmed view that India lost her political and economic independence because her people succumbed to the pressure of greed for gains from trade.

Gandhian pragmatic approach, however, was not for a total rejection of foreign trade. The country must be self-reliant as far as food, cloth and other basic necessities are concerned. Village crafts and industries which can be revived with some effort for their intrinsic merit and their other useful aspects must be given protection. However, goods which are important from people's welfare point of view and which cannot be produced at home, may be imported. As he says, "I have never been an advocate of prohibition of all things foreign because they are foreign. My economic creed is a complete taboo in respect of all foreign commodities whose importation is likely to prove harmful to our indigenous interest. This means that we may not in any circumstance import a commodity that can be adequately supplied from our own country".[55] Thus holistic welfare is the supreme consideration and trade must be subservient to it.

In order to avoid a narrow interpretation of the doctrine of *Swadeshi*, Gandhiji wrote, "Even *swadeshi*, like any other good thing, can be ridden to death if it is made a fetish. That is a danger which must be guarded against. To reject foreign manufacture merely because they are foreign and to go on wasting national time and money in the promotion in one's country of manufacture for which it is not suited would be criminal folly and a negation of the *Swadeshi* spirit".[56]

The Dynamics of Change, Trusteeship, and Satyagraha

Gandhiji dreamt of *'Ramaraj'* on earth based on the values of truth and non-violence. The fulfilment of life lies in constantly moving towards this ideal state, even though it may not be perfectly attainable like the Euclid's point. The movement towards the ideal state, however, is not a mechanical process. Change is the result of a harmonious integration of inner change in man by conscious efforts and outer change in the structures, institutions and organisations influencing man's life. It requires a conscious transformation in man as well as change in outer structure. There is a two-way relationship between change in economic structures and change in man. (Transformation in the individual is at the centre of all the Gandhian thought.) Man must awake to the totality lying dormant within him and live his understanding in relationships. The economic behaviour of the holistic man as a consumer, producer, employer, worker must undergo a revolutionary change based on the basic principles of truth, non-violence, non-stealing, non-possession, bread labour and Swadeshi etc. Self-effacement instead of self-aggrandisement, love instead of aggression, cooperation instead of competition, must become the values of life. Restructuring and reorganisation of outer economic life as spelt out in Gandhiji's constructive programme must go on simultaneously with transformation in man. The right structures help man in his transformation and provide less scope for the operation of violence within him. Gandhiji held that it was foolish to dream of systems so perfect that people would no longer need to be good. He, therefore, contemplated a system so simple that people would no longer need to be bad. The right structures, however, can be created and sustained only when a conscious transformation in the individual takes place side by side. The best of structures may be polluted and destroyed, if man does not become free of the 'pollution' and violence lying within him. Gandhiji thus places a responsibility upon man as he takes him to be capable of bringing about a conscious transformation in himself.

To Gandhiji, non-violence is the force of human evolution. All human action must spring from non-violence and non-violent structures must be created in all walks of life for peace, progress and prosperity. Non-violence is soul-force which is capable of eradicating all that is evil in the world. In its most active form, non-violence becomes *'Satyagraha'*. According to Gandhiji, *Satyagraha* is the firm and fearless adherence to Truth, even in the face of death, without bearing any ill will towards the evil doer. *Satyagraha* is an attempt to awaken the Truth in the heart of the wrong doer through persuasion, self-sacrifice, and self-suffering. The *Satyagrahi* does not try to suppress or liquidate his opponent through the exertion of force of any form. The evil doer is looked at as an extension of one's own self and, therefore, there is no attempt to harm him in any way, except a sincere and fearless action to enlighten the Truth in him through self-sacrifice. *Satyagraha* is, thus, elevating both for the evil-doer as well as the *Satyagrahi*. "It is never the intention of a *satyagrahi* to embarrass the wrong doer. The appeal is never to his fear; it is, must be always to his heart. The satyagrahi's object is to convert, not to coerce, the wrong doers".[57] Satyagraha may be practised by the individuals or groups of individuals in order to bring about any desired change in the economic structure of a society.

Gandhiji's views stand in sharp contrast to those of Marx on the process of change. Marx borrowed from Hegel the method of dialectics and applied it to the material world instead of the world of ideas. All social change, according to Marx, was a matter of material and economic forces. Every epoch of history was marked by antagonistic forces, the division of society into classes engaged in struggle for power. The classes were determined by the modes of production, exchange and distribution. Thus all history, the social changes and political revolutions are ultimately, the result of economic factors.

The modern capitalistic economic system has not done away with class antagonisms. It has established the bourgeoisie, the class of the oppressors on the one side and the proletariate, the class of the oppressed on the other side. Since change is inherent in the system, the oppressed class will overthrow the oppressors through a violent revolution and capture both economic and political power. According to Marx, this process of change is mechanical and inevitable. The inevitability of the process of change led Marx to give a clarion call to the workers of the world to unite, intensify the class struggle and overthrow the capitalist class with all their might. Violence is, thus, inherent in the Marxian system. All change is the result of violence.

Gandhiji, on the other hand, appeals to the higher, creative force of love in man in order to bring about the desired transformation in society in contrast to the fanning of violence, hatred and jealousy in man. Gandhiji was profoundly moved by the poverty and miserable condition of the masses due to the centralisation of the economic power in the hands of the capitalist class. He enunciated the Theory of Trusteeship in order to bring about the required change in a non-violent way.

To Gandhiji, trusteeship is a way of life, rather than just a method to achieve a particular end. According to his holistic approach, everything on this earth belongs to God and is from God. Therefore, it was for His people as a whole, not for a particular individual. Everybody on this earth has a natural right to at least the basic necessities of life, just like the birds and the beasts have. If, somehow, an individual had more than his proportionate share, he was a trustee of that portion for God's people. As Gandhiji wrote, "Supposing I have come by a fair amount of wealth either by way of legacy, or by means of trade and industry, I must know that all that wealth does not belong to me; what belongs to me is the right to an honourable livelihood, no better than that enjoyed by millions of others. The rest of my wealth belongs to the community and must be used for the welfare of community".[58]

Gandhiji was a believer in the primacy not only of mind but also of spirit in him over matter unlike Marx who placed matter over mind. History of mankind is not merely a plaything of environmental and material conditions; the soul-force in man can change the course of history and give it the requisite thrust and direction by changing the material and environmental conditions. Man has the capability to rise above his passions and act according to the call of the spirit. As he described, "The essential difference between man and the brute is that the former can respond to the call of the spirit in him, can rise superior to the passions that he owns in common with the brute and, therefore, superior to selfishness and violence, which belong to the brute nature and not to the immortal spirit of man".[59]

The path of love and non-violence demands that the class of capitalists and the landlords must be persuaded to adopt a just and humane attitude and use their wealth, talents and capabilities for the benefit of the workers and the peasants, according to the spirit of trusteeship. If persuasion through dialogue, discussion and negotiations fails, Satyagraha may be exercised to rouse the spirit of the oppressor through self-suffering. The bond of unity, on the other side, puts a responsibility on the satyagrahi to eschew every form of violence, hatred and ill will. "If I would recognise the fundamental equality, as I must, of the capitalist and the labour, I must not aim at his destruction, I must strive for his conversion".[60] Violence according to Gandhiji, can never usher in non-violence, non-exploitation and equality. Violence always breeds violence. "For experience convinces me that permanent good can never be the outcome of untruth and violence".[61]

In the Marxian system, the proletariat overthrows the bourgeoisie and captures the means of production and political power through a bloody revolution. However, after the dictatorship of the proletariat is established, most heinous crimes are committed in the name of suppressing the remnants of the bourgeoisie. Centralisation of power, economic or political, kills human freedom and individuality. The state becomes an instrument of violence, poverty, inequalities of income, unemployment and oppression reappear on the scene. As observed by Gandhiji, "The State represents violence in a concentrated and organised form. The individual has a soul, but as the state is a soulless machine, it can never be weaned from violence to which it owes its very existence".[62] He further asserts, "It is my firm conviction that if the State suppressed capitalism by violence, it will be caught in the coils of violence itself and fail to develop non-violence at any time".[63] As the world situation stands today, the prophecy made by Gandhiji has come out to be true.

Capital and labour are not antagonistic forces. They are meant to work in cooperation with each other for the benefit of all. If the capitalists realise their responsibilities as trustees and labour awakens to its dignity and pride, the class struggle can be ended for ever. Gandhian holistic approach upholds that creative force of non-violence which works in every human being, if activised, can end all antagonism and establish a non-exploitative, egalitarian economic order on earth, ensuring peace, progress and prosperity to mankind.

Practicability of Gandhian Holistic Economics

Transformation in man is at the centre of Gandhian economics. Is it possible for man to bring about transformation in himself? Can he rise from the level of the matter to the level of the spirit? Will he be able to give up pursuit of selfishness, control his animal passions and adopt an alternative life-style based on truth and non-violence? It seems that in the present day world where a race for more and more material possession is going on, where darkness prevails and violence rules, it is not possible for man to transform himself and become non-violent.

According to Gandhian paradigm man is both matter and spirit. Matter makes him fragmented leading to violence in life. Spiritual awareness gives him a holistic world-view and activises non-violence in him. There is always a struggle raging in man between the powers of darkness and of light, between evil and good. As long as man succumbs to the pressure of matter, he is violent but as soon as he awakes to the spirit in him he becomes non-violent. Gandhiji has the conviction that each man has an inherent capacity to free himself from the bondage of matter and grow into the dimension of the spirit, to rise from violence to non-violence. As soon as a human-being makes a determination and starts practising self-control he starts growing into the dimension of the spirit. The philosophy of non-violence is not simply a dream, it is capable of being put into practice even by ordinary individuals. Replying to his critics, Gandhiji had said, "I am not a visionary. I claim to be a practical idealist. The religion of non-violence is not meant merely for 'Rishis' and saints. It is meant for the common man as well".[64] Gandhiji feels that the human race has the responsibility of abiding by the law of non-violence. It may be difficult to practice self-control, awaken the spirit and follow the path of non-violence, but it is not impossible. Though the path of non-violence is strait and narrow, yet it is not untrekkable. The real test of the strength of man lies in following the path of non-violence and not in waging war on others.

If we look at history, we find sufficient proof of the practicability of the principle of non-violence. Man has been steadily progressing from violence to non-violence. Man was first a cannibal then he became a hunter and later he took to agriculture. From being a wanderer, he settled down to a civilised stable life, founded villages and towns and from member of a family he became member of a community and a nation. Thus the history of mankind is a history of evolution of man. Gandhiji holds the view that all these are "signs of progressive *ahimsa* and diminishing *himsa*".

Love is the law of life. Where there is love there is life, hatred leads to destruction. The fact that mankind persists show that the cohesive force of love is greater than the disruptive force of hatred. There will be no life, the moment the centrifugal force becomes greater than the centripetal. Gandhiji thus discovered that love is the law of life. In fact, law of love is being practised in our daily life even without our being conscious of it. It is reflected in the mother's love for her child, in mutual trust and cooperation, friendship and fellow feeling. Little quarrels of millions of families in their daily lives are resolved through love and understanding. The natural working of the law of love is taken for granted and therefore does not go in the record of history. Gandhiji says, "History is really a record of every interruption of the even working of the force of love or of the soul — soul-force being natural is not noted in history".[65]

Nature does not stand the violation of the law of love. Whenever evil increases and the balance between the various components of the holistic plan is disturbed, natural forces appear to restore the balance. Sometimes nature may become terrible in order to restore the law of love. Gandhiji is therefore, of the confirmed view, "Either man takes to *Ahimsa* or rushes to his doom". If man does not transform and take to the path of non-violence, life on earth stands endangered.

Human history is full of examples of such individuals who were born as ordinary human beings but who through sheer devotion and practice were able to grow spiritually and ultimately merge into the supreme power God. Buddha, Christ, Nanak, Mahommad, Kabir, Meera, Ramkrishna are to name a few who have shown the spiritual heights attainable by a human being. Mahatma Gandhi is another elevated soul of modern era who lived for truth and non-violence and ultimately laid his life for the love of mankind. Gandhiji claims no special divinity in himself and holds the conviction that every human being is capable of transforming his life on the principles of truth. "My preachings and teachings are not emotional or unpractical, for I teach what is ancient and strive to practice what I preach. And I claim that what I practice is capable of being practised by all, because I am a very ordinary mortal open to the same temptations and liable to the same weaknesses as the least among us".[66]

Transformation is becoming free of the slavery of one's narrow material self, rising above the currents of passions or purification of mind so that the light of Supreme Truth may reflect through a human being. Religions all over the world have suggested various paths for realisation of the truth. According to Indian philosophy, *Gyan Yog, Raj Yog, Bhakti Yog, Karam Yog* are some of the main paths for realisation of the ultimate reality. Schumacher in his book *A Guide for the Perplexed* gives the message that there do exist educational processes by which the "inner self" of any human being may be transformed. Gandhiji had suggested identification with all that exists for realising the truth, since truth is all pervading. In practice, the Gandhian approach leads to the path of love or selfless service to mankind. According to the *Gita*, it is *Nishkam Karm Yog*. Non-violence is the power of God-head or soul-force which if practised is capable of purifying not only the individual, but also those who come in contact with the individual practising non-violence. Practice of non-violence requires self-control and Gandhiji had suggested taking up of certain vows for self-control. He believed in regular prayer, getting in communion with God in all humility, to steer us out of all difficulties. Non-violence is capable of being practised by any individual in day-to-day worldly life, provided one has the understanding, the will, the determination to practice it. There is no need to go to the caves or run to the forests. As a matter of fact, Gandhian path of selfless service cannot be practised in isolation, it requires participation in all the worldly activities whether social, political or economic.

Gandhiji's own life stands as a striking example to prove that transformation in the individual is not a utopian idea and that non-violence is practicable. From the level of an ordinary person with all the worldly weaknesses, through practice of non-violence, self-control and faith in God, Gandhiji rose to the level of 'Mahatma'. Gandhiji's life is his message. His life proves that each one of us is capable of bringing about transformation in our lives. In his own words, "I claim to be no more than an average man with less than average ability. Nor can I claim any special merit for such non-violence or continence as I have been able to reach with laborious research. I have not the shadow of a doubt that any man or woman can achieve what I have, if he or she would make the same effort and would cultivate the same hope and faith".[67] Gandhiji practised what he preached. The goal of Gandhiji's life was self-realisation to attain *Moksha.* He was striving to achieve this goal with all his strength throughout his life. He was forever making experiments with truth and trying to regulate his inner and outer life in the light of truth. As he wanted to identify with the poorest of the poor, he lived a life of utter simplicity. His needs were minimum and his belongings were countable. He was an epitome of humility, fearlessness, compassion and child-like innocence. As he considered life to be one whole, he did not make any compartments between inner and outer, material and spiritual, moral and economic, individual or collective life. He was practising the same principle of non-violence whether he was endeavouring for the independence of India, eradication of poverty, self-sufficiency of villages, removal of untouchability or uplifting the status of women. Again it is the same principle of non-violence which is reflected in his plying the *charkha*, fasting for communal harmony, washing the feet of the lepers or trekking along the riot hit area of Noakhali.

The awakening of soul-force in Gandhiji through the practice of non-violence did not remain limited to his own self only, it awakened the masses and gradually developed into a mass scale non-violent force capable of burning all impurities. Gandhiji revolutionised the psyche of the Indian people and turned the helpless, demoralised, down spirited masses groaning under the weight of British imperialism into fearless, conscious, self-respecting individuals. The people became ready to sacrifice their all to regain their lost independence, resist all aggression and fight all evil and injustice. They were stirred to challenge the brute-force through the soul-force. At Gandhiji's call they stood lathi-blows and hails of bullets in an unflinching manner without resorting to violence. They smilingly resigned their jobs, made a bon-fire of foreign clothes, filled the jails and boldly faced all the atrocities committed on them. This was soul-force in action. Arousing the consciousness of the people, Gandhiji successfully organised many *satyagrahas* at different places on various issues. Champaran *Satyagraha* against the tyranny of white indigo planters, mill workers strike at Ahmedabad, Kisan movements at Kheda, Bardoli and Borsad, *Salt Satyagraha* in 1930 when thousands of marchers along with Gandhiji reached the sea-shore at Dandi and picked up the contraband salt, are some of the examples which prove that the force of non-violence can be successfully organised to move the masses and achieve most difficult tasks. India ultimately won freedom through non-violence creating world history.

Thus, transformation in the individual though difficult is not impossible. In fact non-violence is the only path which is capable of taking us out of the present mess that we have got into. A change in perception from fragmentary to holistic, transformation in the individual, and creation of non-violent structures in different walks of life, is the need and challenge of the day.

NOTES

1. *Young India*, July 17, 1924, *CWMG*, Vol. 24, 1967, p. 396.
2. M.K. Gandhi, *Hind Swaraj*, Ahmedabad, Navjivan Publishing House, 1938, p. 71.
3. *Harijan*, June 13, 1947, *The Message of Mahatma Gandhi*, ed. U.S. Mohan Rao, Ahmedabad, Navjivan Publishing House, 1968, p. 26.
4. Bharatan Kumarappa, (Editor's note), M.K. Gandhi, *Rebuilding Our Villages*, Ahmedabad, Navjivan Publishing House, 1952, pp. iii-iv.
5. *Young India*, March 19, 1931, Quoted in *Gandhi in To-Day's* India, ed. B.C. Das & G.P. Mishra, New Delhi, Ashish Publishing House, 1979, p. 48.
6. G. Thimmaiah, *Economic Role of Government in Gandhian Economics*, Paper in *Gandhi in Today's India* ed. B.C. Das & C.P. Mishra, New Delhi Ashish Publishing House, 1979, p. 160.

7. Shriman Narayan, *Relevance of Gandhian Economics*, Ahmedabad, Navjivan Publishing House, 1970, pp. 128-129.
8. *Harijan*, Jan. 18, 1942 *CWMG*, Vol. 75, 1979, p. 216.
9. *Harijan*, July 28, 1946, *India of My Dreams*, op. cit., p. 99.
10. *Harijan*, Nov. 4, 1939, *CWMG*, Vol. 70, 1977, p. 296.
11. M.K. Gandhi, *The Gospel of Swadeshi*, Bombay, Bharatiya Vidya Bhavan, 1967, p. 1. (ed., Anand T. Hingorani).
12. Ibid., p. 8.
13. M.K. Gandhi, *The Gospel of Swadeshi*, op. cit., p. 5.
14. *Harijan*, Aug. 4, 1946, M.K. Gandhi, *Rebuilding Our Villages*, Ahmedabad, Navjivan Publishing House, ed. Bharatan Kumarappa, 1952, pp. 6-7.
15. *Harijan*, July 26, 1942, Ibid., p. 5.
16. *Harijan*, Nov. 10, 1946, M.K. Gandhi, *India of My Dreams*, comp. R.K. Prabhu, Ahmedabad, Navjivan Publishing House, 1947, pp. 97-98.
17. *CWMG*, Vol. 13, 1964, p. 222.
18. *Young India*, June 18, 1931, *The Gospel of Swadeshi*, ed. Anand T. Hingorani, Bombay, Bhartiya Vidya Bhavan, 1967, p. 76.
19. *Harijan*, July 28, 1946, *India of My Dreams*, op. cit., p. 100.
20. *Harijan*, Nov. 16, 1934, *CWMG*, Vol. 59, 1974, p. 357.
21. *Harijan*, Nov. 30, 1934, *CWMG*, Vol. 59, 1974, p. 414.
22. *Young India*, Aug. 220, 1919, *The Gospel of Swadeshi*, op. cit., p. 20.
23. *Harijan*, Nov. 30, 1934, *CWMG*, Vol. 59, 1974, p. 414.
24. *Young India*, May 13, 1919, *The Gospel of Swadeshi*, op. cit., p. 19.
25. M.K. Gandhi, *Hind Swaraj*, op. cit., p. 96.
26. E.F. Schumacher, *Small is Beautiful*, New Delhi, Radha Krishna, 1977, p. 17.
27. Ibid., p. 31.
28. Ibid., p. 140.
29. *The Gita*, 3.12.
30. *Young India*, Jan. 8, 1925, *CWMG*, Vol. 25, 1967, p. 562.
31. M.K. Gandhi, *Economic and Industrial Life and Relations*, Vol. II, comp. V.B. Kher, Ahmedabad, Navjivan Publishing House, 1957, p. 34.
32. Ibid., p. 38.
33. Quoted in Fritjof Capra, *The Turning Point*, London, Fontana Paperbacks, 1982, p. 214.
34. *Economic and Industrial Life and Relations*, ed. V.B. Kher, op. cit., p. 33 (Vol. 22).
35. Ibid., p. 173.
36. *Harijan*, Nov. 16, 1934, *CWMG*, Vol. 59, 1974, p. 356.
37. *Economic and Industrial Life and Relations* Vol. 2, ed., V.B. Kher, op. cit., p. 38.
38. *Harijan*, Sept. 14, 1935, *CWMG*, Vol. 61, 1975, p. 416.
39. *Harijan*, June 20, 1936, *CWMG*. Vol. 63, 1976, p. 77.
40. B.N. Ganguli, *Gandhi's Social Philosophy*, Delhi, Vikas Publishing House, 1973, p. 295.
41. Amritananda Das, *Foundations of Gandhian Economics*, Calcutta, Allied Publishers, 1979, p. 8.
42. Ibid., p. 8.
43. *Harijan*, Aug. 29, 1936, *CWMG*, Vol. 63, 1976, p. 241.
44. *Harijan*, Feb. 12, 1938, *CWMG*, Vol. 66, 1976, p. 355.
45. *Economic and Industrial Life and Relations*, Vol. 2, ed., V.B. Kher, op. cit., p. 38.

46. *Young India*, Nov. 13, 1924, *Economic and Industrial Life and Relations*, Vol. 2, p. 39.
47. J.D. Sethi, *Gandhi Today*, New Delhi, Vikas Publishing House, 1978, p. 116.
48. M.K. Gandhi, *Constructive Programme*, Ahmedabad, Navjivan Publishing House, 1941, p. 25.
49. *Harijan*, Nov. 2, 1934, M.K. Gandhi, *India of My Dreams*, op. cit., p. 30.
50. *Economic and Industrial Life and Relations*, Vol. 2, op. cit., pp. 167-168.
51. Ibid., p. 168.
52. *Young India*, May 30, 1929, M.K. Gandhi, *Gospel of Swadeshi*, op. cit., p. 71.
53. Quoted in Bepin Behari, *Gandhian Economic Philosophy*, Bombay, Vora and Co. Publishers, 1963, p. 95.
54. *Young India*, Oct. 13, 1921, *CWMG*, Vol. 21, 1966, p. 290.
55. *Young India*, Nov. 15, 1928, M.K. Gandhi, *The Gospel of Swadeshi*, op. cit., p. 68.
56. M.K. Gandhi, *From Yeravda Mandir*, Ahmedabad, Navjivan Publishing House, 1932, p. 43.
57. *Harijan*, Mar. 25, 1939, *CWMG*, Vol. 69, 1977, p. 69.
58. *Harijan*, June 3, 1939, *Economic and Industrial Life and Relations*, Vol. 1, op. cit., (comp. V.B. Kher), p. 157.
59. *Amrit Bazar Patrika*, Aug. 2, 1934, M.K. Gandhi, *India of My Dreams* (comp. R.K. Prabhu), op. cit., p. 27.
60. *Young India*, Mar. 26, 1931, *CWMG*, Vol. 45, 1971, p. 339.
61. *Young India*, Dec. 11, 1924, *CWMG*, Vol. 25, 1967, p. 424.
62. M.K. Gandhi, *Sarvodaya*, ed. Bharatan Kumarappa, Ahmedabad, Navjivan Publishing House, 1954, p. 74.
63. M.K. Gandhi, *Sarvodaya*, ed. Bharatan Kumarappa, Ahmedabad, Navjívan Publishing House, 1954, p. 74.
63. Ibid., p. 74.
64. *Young India*, Aug. 11, 1920, *CWMG*, Vol. 18, Nov. 1965, p. 133.
65. M.K. Gandhi, *Hind Swaraj*, op. cit., pp. 78-79.
66. *Young India*, Dec. 15, 1927, *CWMG*, Vol. 35, Aug. 1969, p. 385.
67. *Harijan*, Oct. 3, 1936. *CWMG*, Vol. 63, Jan. 1976, p. 342.

7

AN OVERVIEW

ECONOMICS IS the outcome of a particular world-view, certain meta-economic factors or postulates regarding the ultimate reality of life, prevailing at a time. The image of the 'self' and the 'non-self', concepts and values arising out of a particular world-view bear upon man's economic behaviour regarding 'ends' and 'means', which in turn is the determinant of the entire fabric of economics, its principles, policy, structure and all the other manifestations.

Modern economics is based upon a fragmentary paradigm. It is universally accepted by all the schools of thought that there is a basic dichotomy between the part and the rest of the world, the 'self' and the 'non-self'. The various constituents of the universe are finite, discrete and mechanistic moving under some kind of force. The world-view that life is in fragments has implied in economic terms as follows:

(a) Man is a material, mechanistic, autonomous being, functioning under the force of wants for the sake of maximising pleasure. Man is, thus, basically a consumer having unlimited wants.
(b) Society is a collection of atomistic beings competing with one another for the pursuit of 'self-interest'.
(c) The purpose of economics is pursuit of materialism, i.e., provisioning of more and more goods and services now or in future for 'betterment', happiness or 'well-being' of man and society.
(d) Growth is material progress measured by the rate of growth of GNP.
(e) The road to material progress is through 'competition' and technological advancement.
(f) Economic problems generated by the pursuit of materialism can be solved by fragmentary methods at the micro or macro levels.

The fragmentary paradigm underlying modern economics is

responsible for giving rise to a world economic crisis. The world today is faced with a number of irrepressible and uncontrollable problems not only at the economic but also at the environmental, political, social and human levels. The economic crisis generated by the pursuit of materialism is multi-faceted involving depletion of scarce world-resources, environmental pollution, ecological imbalance, poverty and hunger, inequalities, exploitation, unemployment, inflation, economic instability, social and political tensions, alienation and dehumanisation. The nature and magnitude of these problems is such that they defy all solutions within the existing frame-work of economics. It is being predicted that the present trends, if unaltered, may soon lead to the collapse of the very industrial system and may even endanger human survival.

The paradigm underlying Gandhian economics is fundamentally different from that which forms the basis of modern economics. Mahatma Gandhi accepts a 'holistic' world-view, taking all life to be vertically and horizontally as one homogeneous whole. He had an immovable faith that 'God alone is', that there is an absolute, unitary, changeless reality which is ever existing and all pervading. He preferred to call this reality which is beyond time, space and causation 'Truth', because nothing is or exists in reality except Truth. Everything living or non-living is a manifestation of the same reality. The various parts in nature, due to the inner thread of unity, are functioning continuously to help each other for the common good of the whole. Life is, therefore, not in parts, but it is one whole. The natural regulating force of Truth does not stand the violation of the principle of unity of life. Treatment of life in fragments, over-emphasis or neglect of any part is bound to create friction, disharmony and imbalance. Whenever such a situation arises, the force of Truth appears in some form or the other to restore order.

A new concept of man emerges from the holistic approach. Man is a part of the whole and has wholeness enfolded within him. He is not simply a limited, material being but he has an unbounded spiritual existence also. Man is potentially divine. He has the capacity to transcend his mechanistic nature, reach higher and higher levels of consciousness and be rooted in Truth.

The purpose of man's life is Truth-realisation, to attain Moksha, the highest and purest state of existence. Since Truth is immanent in everything, Truth realisation requires identification with all that exists, even the meanest of the creation. Gandhiji, thus, suggested the path of

Love or non-violence to reach the goal of Truth. The motivational force for human behaviour is not the pursuit of self-interest but the spirit of 'reducing the self to zero', which is an essential condition for the practice of non-violence.

Economics must be subservient to the basic goal of Truth. Ethics, therefore, cannot be separated from economics. Gandhian economics is a normative science, taking man as he 'ought to be' and not as he 'is'.

The entire Gandhian economic thought is the outcome of an endeavour to realise the Truth through non-violence. The truth of the wholeness of life is adhered to in every field. It may be said that all of Gandhiji's economic ideas grow out of truth, are nurtured by truth and reach the truth. Founded on a holistic world-view and the accompanying values and concepts, Gandhiji has built up an extremely systematic, coherent and logical economic system. There is a philosophical rationale behind every economic idea that has been floated. The validity and justification of the Gandhian economics, its principles, policy, 'ends' and 'means', analysis and structure lies in truth and non-violence arising out of a holistic world-view.

Gandhian economics based on a holistic paradigm and ethical values like truth, non-violence, non-stealing, non-possession, *Brahmacharya*, equality, bread labour, *Swadeshi* and trusteeship, shows a radical departure from modern economics. Gandhiji equates 'well-being' or happiness of man with spiritual or moral elevation, and therefore, maintains that the basic goal of economics is not pursuit of unbounded materialism, but provision of optimal amount of goods and services in order to keep the body and mind in a fit condition so that through service, the highest potentiality of man may be realised. Truth requires that wants should be scientifically explored, pruned and regulated in the light of wholeness. Gandhian economics is, therefore, need-oriented and not want-oriented. Besides fulfilment of needs, Sarvodaya, equality, end of all deprivation and exploitation, creative work for all are some of the other basic 'ends' of holistic economics.

Growth is an ascent of consciousness. Since man is both physical as well as spiritual, and the physical is instrumental in unfolding the spiritual, growth is a function of material as well as moral factors.

Economic ends which are rooted in Truth must be achieved by holistic means only since there is an inviolable connection between the ends and the means. The economic principles underlying Gandhian holistic economics are decentralisation, self-sufficiency, cooperation, equality, *Swadeshi* and trusteeship. The structure of a non-violent economy is composed of a number of decentralised, self-sufficient economic units. The economic unit is able to produce whatever is required with the help of local resources and is contented with whatever has been produced in local surroundings. Mutual help, cooperation and sharing among the various economic units is, however, not ruled out. Gandhiji was opposed to unlimited industrialisation and 'machinery' due to evils inherent in them. He suggested suitable limits to be imposed on them. Not only that, industrialisation and technological advancement must be within limits; the scale of operations must also be small. Technological progress and expansion of scale of production, without the accompanying spiritual advancement, inevitably leads to human degradation. Gandhiji advocated the promotion of handicrafts, village and small-scale industries and suggested that existing local technology must be revived and improved upon. There should be 'production by masses' instead of 'mass production' so that distribution can take place simultaneously with production, in order to ensure equality. Gandhiji was, however, willing to accept a few heavy and large scale industries with high technology in the national interest, provided they are under state control and are subservient to the needs of the village and small industries. He, thus, favoured a harmonious integration of industries with different technologies and capital intensities.

Gandhian holistic economic order proposes to solve the present economic problems and assures humanity a good living, dignity, freedom as well as moral elevation.

The aim of all the Gandhian thought and action is *'Ramaraj'*, a perfect state of peace, prosperity and progress based on the principles of truth and non-violence. This is a state in which the *'Swaraj'* i.e., economic political, social and moral liberation, has been achieved. The fulfilment of life lies in continuously moving towards this state, even though it may not be perfectly attainable like the Euclid's point. Gandhiji laid emphasis on the movement towards the goal rather than the goal itself; the means rather than the ends.

The movement towards the ideal is not a mechanical process, being the result of material and economic forces. Change in Gandhian terms is the result of a harmonious integration of conscious inner transformation in man and change in outer structures. There is a two-way relationship between change in man and change in economic structures. The right structures help man in his transformation by providing less scope for the operation of violence within him.

Transformation in the individual, on the other hand, is essential for the creation and sustenance of right structures.

Transformation in the individual is at the centre of all the Gandhian thought. Man must awake to the Truth, the wholeness lying dormant within him and change the dynamics of his relationships on the basis of Love and non-violence. The economic behaviour of man as a consumer, producer, employer, and worker must undergo a holistic transformation on the principles of truth, non-violence, non-stealing, non-possession, bread labour, equality and trusteeship. 'Self-annihilation' instead of self-aggrandisement, love instead of aggression, cooperation instead of 'competition' must become the values of life. Love or non-violence is the law of human evolution. In its most active form, non-violence becomes *'Satyagraha'*, that is, firm and fearless adherence to Truth, even in the face of death, without bearing any ill-will towards the opponent. *'Satyagraha'* must be practised at the individual or the collective level in order to fight economic evils and bring about any desired change.

Gandhiji believed in the primacy of spirit over matter. History of mankind is not merely a plaything of environmental and material conditions; the soul force in man can change the course of history and give it the required thrust and direction. Man who is potentially divine, has the capability to rise above his passions and act according to the call of the spirit. Transformation in man, a paradigm shift from 'fragmentary' to 'holistic' is the need and challenge of the day.

BIBLIOGRAPHY

Books

Adam Smith, *The Wealth of Nations*, New York, The Modern Library, Random House, Inc., 1937.

A.C. Pigou, *Economics of Welfare*, Fourth Edition, London, Macmillan and Co. Ltd., 1952.

Alfred Marshal, *Principles of Economics*, eighth edition, London, Macmillan and Co. Ltd., 1959.

Amritananda Das, *Foundations of Gandhian Economics*, Calcutta, Allied Publishers Private Ltd., 1979.

Barry Commoner, *The Closing Circle*, New York, Alfred A. Knopt, 1975.

B.C. Das and G.P. Mishra (eds.), *Gandhi in To-Day's India*, New Delhi, Ashish Publishing House, 1979.

B.N. Ganguli, *Gandhi's Social Philosophy*, Delhi, Vikas Publishing House, 1973.

Bepin Behari, *Gandhian Economic Philosophy*, Bombay, Vora and Co., Publishers Pvt. Ltd., 1968.

Bertrand Russel, *History of Western Philosophy*, London, George Allen and Unwin Ltd., 1957.

The Bible.

Brihadaranykopanishad.

B.L. Atreya, *Practical Vedant*, Lucknow, Rama Tirth Pratisthan, 1966.

Charles Darwin, *The Origin of Species*, sixth edition, New York, The New American Library , 1872.

D.G. Tendulkar, *Mahatma*, New Delhi, Publications Division, Government of India, 1951.

D.S. Kothari, *Some Thoughts on Science and Religion*, Shri Raj Krishen Jain Charitable Trust, New Delhi, 1977.

Dada Dharmadhikari, *Ahimsak Kranti Ki Prakriya*, Kashi, Akhil Bhartiya Sarvseva Sangh, 1962.

David F. Ross, and Mahendra S. Kanthi, *Gandhian Economics*, Bangalore, Prasad Publications, 1983.

Deendayal Upadhyaya, *The Integral Approach*, New Delhi, Deendayal Research Institute, 1979.

Donella H. Meadows, et al. *The Limits to Growth*, New York, Potomac Associates, 1974.

E.F. Schumacher, *Small is Beautiful*, New Delhi, Radha Krishan, New Delhi, 1977.

——, *A Guide for the Perplexed*, London, ABACUS edition, Sphere Books Ltd., 1978.

——, *Good Work*, New York, Harper and Row Publishers, 1980.

Fred Hirsch, *The Social Limits to Growth*, London, Routledge and Kegan Paul, 1977.

Fritjof Capra, *The Turning Point*, London, Fontana Paperbacks, 1983.

——, *The Tao of Physics*, Fontana/Collins, 1976.

Gunnar Myrdal, *Economic Theory and Under-developed Regions*, London, Gerald Duckworth and Co. Ltd., 1957.

The Gita.

Hazel Henderson, *Creating Alternative Futures*, New York, Berkley Publishing Corporation, 1978.

I.K. Taimni, *Science and Occultism*, Madras, The Theosophical Publishing House, 1974.

Indu Tikekar, *Integral Revolution*, Varanasi, Sarva Seva Sangh Prakashan, 1970.

Ishavasyopanishad.

James Bonar, *Philosophy and Political Economy*, second impression, London, George Allen and Unwin Ltd., 1967.

Jayaprakash Narayan, *Total Revolution*, Varanasi, Sarva Seva Sangh Prakashan, 1975.

J.C. Kumarappa, *Why the Village Movement*, Kashi, Akhil Bharat Sarva Seva Sangh Prakashan, 1960.

——, *Economy of Permanence*, Varanasi, Sarva Seva Sangh Prakashan, 1984.

J.D. Sethi, *Gandhi Today*, New Delhi, Vikas Publishing House Pvt. Ltd., 1978.

J. Krishnamurti, *Freedom from the Known*, edited by Mary Lutyens, New Delhi, B.I. Publications, 1975.

J.K. Mehta, *Gandhian Thought*, New Delhi, Ashish Publishing House, 1985.

John M. Keynes, *The General Theory of Employment, Interest and Money*, London, Macmillan & Co. Ltd., 1960.

John Kenneth Galbraith, *The Affluent Society*, Bombay Lalvani Publishing House, 1970 (First Indian Edition).

John Ruskin, *Unto This Last*, London, George Allen and Unwin Ltd.,1960.

Joseph A. Schumpeter, *History of Economic Analysis*, fourth printing, London, George Allen and Unwin Ltd., 1961.

Karl Marx, *Capital*, Vol.1, Moscow, Foreign Languages Publishing House.

——, and Frederick Engels, *Selected Works*, Volume 1, Moscow, Foreign Languages Publishing House, 1951.

Kathopanishad.

Ken Wilber (ed.), *The Holographic Paradigm and Other Paradoxes*, London, Shambhala Publications, 1982.

Kenneth E. Boulding, *Human Values and Economic Policy*, New York University Press, 1967.

Krishna Chaitanya, *Gandhi's Quest of Being in Becoming*, New Delhi, Gandhi Peace Foundation, 1977.

Lawrence G. Hines, *Environmental Issues*, New York, Norton and Company, Inc., 1973.

Lewis H. Haney, *History of Economic Thought*, fourth edition, New York, The Macmillan Company, 1964.

Lionel Robbins, *An Essay on the Nature and Significance of Economic Science*, second edition, Macmillan and Co. Ltd., 1949.

Madhu Dandvate, *Marx and Gandhi*, Bombay, Popular Prakashan Pvt. Ltd., 1977.

Mahadev Prasad, *Social Philosophy of Mahatma Gandhi*, Gorakhpur, Vishwavidyalaya Prakashan, 1958.

Mahadev Desai, *The Gita According to Gandhi*, Ahmedabad, Navjivan Publishing House, 1956.

Maitri Upanishad.

Mark A. Lutz, and Kenneth Lux, *The Challenge of Humanistic Economics*, California, The Benjamin/Cummings Publicity Company, 1979.

M.K. Gandhi, *Hind Swaraj or Indian Home Rule*, Ahmedabad, Navjivan Publishing House, 1938.

——, *From Yeravda Mandir*, Ahmedabad, Navjivan Publishing House, 1932.

——, *An Autobiography or The Story of My Experiments with Truth*, Ahmedabad, Navjivan Publishing House, 1940.

——, *Constructive Programme: Its Meaning and Place*, Ahmedabad, Navjivan Publishing House, 1941.

——, *Ethical Religion*, Ahmedabad, Navjivan Publishing House, 1968.

——, *Rebuilding Our Villages*, Ahmedabad, Navjivan Publishing House, 1969.

——, *Sarvodaya*, Ahmedabad, Navjivan Publishing House, 1969.

——, *Toward Non-Violent Socialism*, Ahmedabad, Navjivan Publishing House, 1957.

——, *India of My Dreams*, Ahmedabad, Navjivan Publishing House, 1957.

——, *The Gospel of Swadeshi*, Bombay, Bhartiya Vidya Bhavan, 1967.

——, *My God*, Ahmedabad, Navjivan Publishing House, 1962.

——, *Capital and Labour*, Bombay, Bhartiya Vidya Bhavan, 1970.

——, *Voluntary Poverty*, Ahmedabad, Navjivan Publishing House, 1961.

——, *Truth is God*, Ahmedabad, Navjivan Publishing House, 1959.

——, *All Men are Brothers*, New York, Columbia University Press, 1958.

——, *Ashram Observances in Action*, Ahmedabad, Navjivan Publishing House, 1959.

——, *Economic and Industrial Life and Relations*, Ahmedabad, Navjivan Publishing House, 1959.

——, *Service Before Self*, Bombay, Bhartiya Vidya Bhavan, 1971.

——, *Khadi*, Ahmedabad, Navjivan Publishing House, 1955.

——, *The Collected Works of Mahatma Gandhi*, New Delhi, The Publications Division, Ministry of Information and Broadcasting, Government of India.

Nirmal Kumar Bose, *Selections from Gandhiji*, Ahmedabad, Navjivan Publishing House, 1957.

Paul A. Samuelson, *Economics*, eleventh edition, Auckland, McGraw-Hill, 1980.

Ramashray Roy, *Gandhi Soundings in Political Philosophy*, Delhi, Chanakya Publications, 1984.

Ram K. Vepa, *New Technology: A Gandhian Concept*, New Delhi, Gandhi Book House, 1975.

R.H. Tawney, *The Acquisitive Society*, Great Britain, Wheatsheaf Books Ltd., 1982.

R.R. Diwakar, *Is Not Gandhi The Answer?*, Bombay, Bhartiya Vidya Bhavan, 1966.

——, *Gandhi: A Practical Philosopher*, Bombay, Bhartiya Vidya Bhavan, 1965.

The Republic of Plato, London, Everyman's Library, J.M. Dent and Sons Ltd., 1935.

Richard B. Gregg, *A Discipline for Non-violence*, Ahmedabad, Navjivan Publishing House, 1941.

Robert L. Heilbroner, *The Worldly Philosophers*, U.S.A., Pelican Books, 1983.

——, *Business Civilization in Decline*, London, Marion Boyars, 1976.

——, *Economic Means and Social Ends*, New Jersey, Prentice-Hall, Inc., 1969.

Romain Rolland, *Mahatma Gandhi*, New Delhi, Publications Division, Government of India, 1976.

Romesh Diwan, Mark Lutz, *Essays in Gandhian Economics*, New Delhi, Gandhi Peace Foundation, 1985.

Shriman Narayan, *Gandhi: The Man and His Thought*, New Delhi, Publications Division, Government of India, 1968.

——, *Relevance of Gandhian Economics*, Ahmedabad, Navjivan Publishing House, 1970.

Shanti S. Gupta, *The Economic Philosophy of Mahatma Gandhi*, Delhi, Ashok Publishing House.

T. Scitovsky, *The Joyless Economy*, Oxford, Oxford University Press, 1976.

Taittriya Upanishad.

U.S. Mohan Rao (ed.), *The Message of Mahatma Gandhi*, New Delhi, Publications Division, Government of India, 1968.

Unto Tahtinen, *The Core of Gandhi's Philosophy*, New Delhi, Abhinav Publications, 1979.

Vimala Thakar, *Towards Total Transformation*, Ahmedabad, New Order Publishing Co., 1970.

——, *Spirituality and Social Action*, Berkeley, Vimala Programs, California, 1984.

Vivekananda, *Jnana-Yoga*, Calcutta, The Sun Lithography Co., 1976.

V.K.R.V. Rao, *Indian Socialism*, New Delhi, Concept Publishing Company, 1982.

V.C. Chappell, *The Philosophy of David Hume*, New York, The Modern Library, Random House, Inc., 1963.
V.M. Dandekar and N. Rath, *Poverty in India*, Bombay, Indian School of Political Economy Publications, 1971.
Vadilal Lallubhai Mehta, *Equality Through Trusteeship and Full Employment*, Bombay, Bhartiya Vidya Bhavan, 1977.
W.L. Davidson, *Political Thought in England: The Utilitarians from Bentham to Mill*, London, Oxford University Press, 1942.

Reports, Journals and Publications

Economic and Political Weekly, Bombay.
Gandhi Marg, New Delhi.
Going Beyond the Intellect: A Gandhian Approach to Scientific Education, Gandhi Peace Foundation, New Delhi.
Harijan, Ahmedabad.
International Labour Office, *Employment, Growth and Basic Needs: A One-World Problem*, New York, Praegar, 1977.
Science Dynamics — A Newly Emerging Paradigm, Gandhi Peace Foundation, New Delhi.
The World Bank Annual Report, The World Bank, Washington, 1984.
The World Bank, *World Development Report*, Oxford, 1984.
Young India, Ahmedabad.

INDEX